THREE
LETTERS

a memoir

by A.L Mengel

COPYRIGHT DISCLAIMER

A.L. MENGEL'S BOOKSHELF

Ashes

The Quest for Immortality

The Blood Decanter

War Angel

Ballet of The Crypt Dancer

&

The Wandering Star

The Europa Effect

Colonia Volume One – The Arrival of Destiny

Colonia Volume Two – Battle of the Trinity

&

The Mortician

Mona Lisa, Becoming a Ghost

&

#Writestorm

#PaintTheWorld

BOOK REVIEWS

"...entirely unique in the approach A.L. Mengel takes in crafting a supernatural tale as old as death itself"

— READER'S FAVORITE (**Mona Lisa, Becoming a Ghost**)

"A brilliant tour-de-force through the psyche of immortals and a welcome addition to the series of novels by A.L. Mengel"

— AMAZON (**The Blood Decanter**)

"...hypnotic...brilliant how the author used objects - like a mirror, a candelabra, or a piece of music - to move the story from one time period to another..."

— BARNES AND NOBLE (**The Mortician**)

"The author's exquisite descriptions of outer space will leave the reader spellbound..."

— GOODREADS (**The Arrival of Destiny**)

"...will raise questions about purpose and sanity, but never strays from the final message – that imperfection is never absolute."

— AMAZON (**Ashes**)

VIDEO STORYTELLING (VLOGS)

#Haunted Paranormal Vlog Series (2021-current)

#TheEraOf Introspective Vlog Series – How art learns from life (2019-current)

#MarchofTheWriters Annual Vlog Series (2021-current)

View A.L. Mengel's Vlog Series on his YouTube channel

BOOK TOURS

Take a Journey Book Tour (2018)

The Stardust Tour – Be My Ghost Book Tour (2022-2023)

FROM THE AUTHOR

To the Wanderers and the Crypt Dancers,

There's something about the stepping stones that I can't get out of my mind. Not that I would want to, anyway. For years now, I have envisioned our life journey as a path of stepping stones reaching out towards the horizon. In many visions I have, the path leads outwards through a vast, infinite ocean. As for me, a seemingly endless body of water like that is a representation of the mysteries which lie ahead.

What we don't know, quiet often, is how we will make it to that next stone, the upcoming chapter in our lives. Also, the stones closest to shore can be most slippery, and hard to stand on, as the waves crash against them, and are covered with water and sea spray. As the stones reach further outwards, the waters tend to calm down, and we have steadier footing. Still, there are often others in our lives who help us get to that next stone, the next step in our journey. Those people are the angels, the foundations of our lives, and they help us navigate the slippery stones close to the shore.

This book was written based on the encouragement of those foundational people in my life who not only had a great hand in the development of me as a person, but also helped me overcome the uncertainty, which was a part of my life, and often still is.

I have also procrastinated with this book for many years. *Three Letters* was one of the first books that I started, back in 2007 or so, and I always kept putting it away so I could write the next novel that I was inspired to write. *Three Letters* sat, as the story marinated, became richer and more complex, as my writing skills were honed and sharpened, as I had many discussions with numerous people involved to gain many different perspectives of what happened. I wrote scenes from my infancy, which I have no recollection of, but the memories are those of my parents, and the stories which they told me, and the feelings that they felt.

In my childhood, I started to harvest my own memories and feelings, as I built my memories into a protagonist, and crafted my parents, and my mother in particular, as heroes of the story. As I work on my upcoming novel *The Spirit Guide,* I think a lot about serendipity. And those little moments that capture our imagination, sometimes years later, as we believe *yes, that was meant to happen. That was definitely part of my journey.* And we discover the many puzzle pieces that make up who we are as people. This memoir is just that type of story.

While I hope you enjoy the story, please know that all of us carry those crosses of uncertainty. We each have one to hold with us throughout our lives, and although there may be some that have the ability to put the cross down, many do not, and that, in no way, should limit our potential as human beings, and how we can make an impact on the world. So now, dear readers, I invite you to read the story that has been many years in the making. As the pages continue to turn, as you get to know the protagonist, keep in mind, that protagonist is me.

For this is my story.

With much love,

A. L. Mengel

THREE
LETTERS

My Personal Journey with Phenylketonuria (PKU)

a memoir of one of the first PKU Babies to be placed on an experimental treatment program for the metabolic disorder

by A.L. Mengel

award-winning author

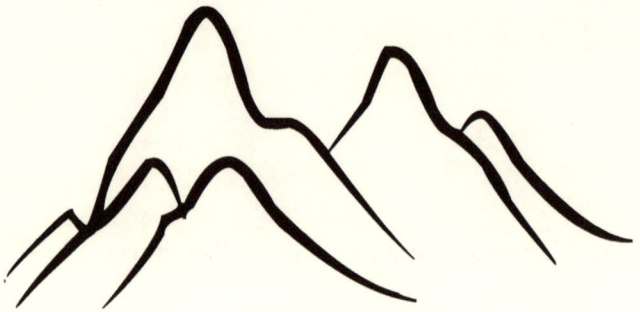

FOR MY MOTHER, MY FATHER, AND MY
FAMILY

"Stories are better teachers than theories." — ROBERT MOSS

"With *The Fablemans*, it wasn't about metaphor, it was about memory." — STEVEN SPIELBERG

TABLE OF CONTENTS

YOU ARE SPECIAL

YOU ARE UNIQUE

THERE IS NO ONE ELSE QUITE LIKE YOU

WHO AM I?

WHY AM I HERE?

WHERE AM I GOING?

THE THREE LETTERS

STILLNESS *and* MOVEMENT

Time was never on my side.

The odds forever stacked against me.

Yet still I remain.

I wonder, am I merely a shell of the human I was meant to be?

Or is this everything I was to become?

I stand at the door and knock, but there comes no answer, I cannot move, yet time does not sit idle.

The sounds of daily life are drowned out by the thoughts others let slip from their control, written on their faces as they trudge from moment to moment, a whispering remnant of time, but not their own person.

Until time, despite our reluctance, our hesitation, places enough distance between us and our thoughts, that we may find the strength to

rise once more . . .

- ROBERT CANO, sci-fi and fantasy author

PART ONE

YOU ARE SPECIAL

BUTTERFLY

A cosmic dance amidst galaxy dreams

A tapestry of interstellar breaths

Destinations across forgotten stars

It soars

But silence

And pastels

Form wings…

- A.L. MENGEL, sci fi and supernatural author

CHAPTER ONE

IT WAS MOSTLY MY MOTHER who carried the cross of uncertainty in those days.

It was her, my father, and my family.

I did not pick it up until I was older, it seemed. I was born at a time when the rare genetic condition, *Phenylketonuria,* known to the medical community and those who have the condition as "PKU", was still quite mysterious, even to the doctors. There were studies in the past where those with PKU had been afflicted with severe mental challenges and limited brain development, inhibited thinking, and communicating, along with experiencing a myriad of major health problems and life challenges.

Still, while writing this, decades later, despite the advancements in medical science, there remains no cure. Advancements, yes. But no true cure.

I was one of the first children to be placed on a then-experimental treatment program to allow for normal brain and central nervous system development, but it was so new at that time that doctors did not know if it would be effective.

There were many uncertainties, multiple unknowns.

Would Andrew develop normally? Or was he destined to live a life of mental hinderance?

There was the concern I would be like those who had the condition were, prior to Dr. Robert Guthrie's discovery of a simple test; a prick of the heel of a two-week-old infant, for a drop of blood, to identify if there was the presence of a strange condition that was afflicting people, casting them into mental anguish and limitation; and, to determine if the liver was complete and normal…or not.

This mysterious disorder.

Phenylketonuria. It is inherited from a recessive gene, in which the liver lacks an enzyme, the one responsible for the breakdown of protein. Yet, when the protein is initially consumed, nothing happens. The baby would be seemingly normal. Until...the symptoms begin.

They come quietly.

Like a thief in the night.

As one of the first babies to be breast-fed while on the PKU treatment program, my mother, along with my father, insisted I get the cerebrosides for proper brain development, which the PKU synthetic formulas did not contain. This was an effort which the doctors at the time I was born would not recommend.

"I was completely grief-stricken," my mother said, writing a paper on her experience shortly after I was born. "The fact of PKU was quite easy to accept in comparison to this pronouncement that denied me my right to nurture, nourish, comfort, and love my child in the way I felt was best. About the third day of Andrew's hospitalization, when the initial shock had dulled, I began hand-expressing milk for my own comfort as well as to be sure I would still have milk in case there would ever be a day when Andrew might return to my breast. My emotional state, added to my lack of sleep and nourishment, had already caused my milk supply to diminish considerably."

I was just a baby when she wrote those words.

I recently read them and felt their heartache.

She knew that my mind could not develop normally unless it had the necessary cerebrosides, which aid normal brain development. They are present in human breastmilk, but not in any of the special formulas which I was required to drink by the medical teams.

"Your mother used to express the milk from her breasts," my father said, in recent years, when I was researching this book. "She initially did it at the hospital when you were born. And then in the first few days after you were at home. She used to freeze it and would measure it when she gave it to you. Along with a bunch of vegetables and things we could give you when you were old enough."

A few days after the chat with my father, when I had a conversation with my mother, separately, and she confirmed. "The doctors refused to recommend it," she said. "But how could your mind develop normally without these necessary proteins? Would you be able to discover your full potential?"

I shifted the phone from one ear to the other, and nodded, even though she could not see me, being over a thousand miles away.

"Dad told me that I was one of the first PKU babies to be placed on this treatment," I said.

"Yes, yes. You were. We knew so little. The doctors knew so little. The diet they placed you on, Andrew, had just been created. The doctors insisted you be placed on it if you had any hope for a chance of a normal life, but they didn't know if it would work. No one knew. But there were no other options. And the alternative...was the effects of your PKU. You could have very well been severely mentally disabled, perhaps in one of my institutions."

"Yes, it could have been far worse. But what about breast feeding? The doctors wouldn't recommend it?"

"Not breastfeeding, no. There was too much protein."

"But you guys did it anyway."

"Yes, we did. Your father was traveling a lot in those days. But we worked with the doctors, and I made sure to pump the breast milk out and measure it when I gave it to you. I also made sure to breast feed you, not as a complete part of your nourishment, of course, because of your PKU. You couldn't have the protein. But sometimes, I would breastfeed you so there was the mother child connection, in that this way of feeding you becomes a deep and spiritual bond."

"Why did you go against the doctor's advice?"

"There's a closeness between mother and child that develops through breastfeeding. And really, because you needed the cerebrosides for your brain development. We wanted you to reach your full potential. And I did a lot of research back then. I was part of *La Leche League*, which was a group of mothers who came together to discuss how they could breast feed their babies when they are born with these types of conditions. where it becomes difficult or impossible to breast feed. We determined ways that it could be done."

"Wow," I said. "That is amazing."

"We had to make sure that your brain developed properly, Andrew. I saw too much with Phenylketonuria where people's lives were essentially crushed with horrendous mental challenges. And when the doctors said they had this new treatment, there was hope for you. But your father and I wanted you to have the best future that you could have."

Before those days, when she carried me, and even when I was born, she didn't know. Neither did my father. Or anyone else in the family, for that matter.

No one knew what was going to happen when I entered the world; when I was born, when I promptly peed on the doctor.

No one could have been prepared for the news.

My parents, especially, picked up and carried the cross together; they were forced to, heavy as it may have been, without warning. They had their lives; they juggled the demands of the world, while raising their first-born son, my older brother, and were a loving family.

But then I entered the picture and shifted the landscape.

I was born, I was tested, and their lives were turned upside down.

My father requested a transfer at work, completely changing his career path, so he could travel less and be home more often, and so we could move out of state, to live near a special PKU clinic which was well-versed in the care of the condition – as informed as a clinic could be in those days of uncertainty.

My father did that because Andrew needed special care.

My mother continued to insist that I should be breast-fed to help with brain development. Yet doctors sternly warned against it, and she spent hours pumping the milk from her breasts, freezing it, and measuring it out specifically to mix with my medically prescribed formula.

My family wanted me to have some natural mind and nervous system development, without exceeding my daily allotment of protein that my body could tolerate, as my liver did not have the necessary enzyme to break down any food that contained protein.

It was like balancing on a tight rope.

I had to be monitored for any symptoms that may arise. My blood was tested regularly to monitor the levels of the toxic substance phenylalanine in my blood; if it built to levels which my body could not tolerate, and prior to having the heel prick test, I became a fussy baby.

"You were inconsolable," my mother told me, decades later, as I was on the phone with her, researching this book. I could hear the hurt in her voice, from a mother who loved her baby so much, yet felt helpless, unable to comfort her child. "You cried, and you cried. There was nothing I could do to stop it, Andrew."

The uncertainty came.

Their world was indeed turned upside down.

No longer were we a regular family.

Two short weeks had passed since my birth, and at that time, there was something potentially devastating on the menu. What was this strange condition? This inherited metabolic disorder that threatened the development of the mind and central nervous system.

Phenylketonuria?

My parents questioned the doctors; they studied the limited history of the rare condition and started the long journey of raising me. PKU. It couldn't even be pronounced, really, and we gave it to our *son*?

My parents were both carriers of the recessive gene, and when two carriers of the gene reproduce, there is a twenty-five percent chance of PKU positive offspring. I fell in the unlucky square on the genetics table. My brother and my sister are also carriers.

Everyone took a role in my care; my brother and sister stepped in, when they were old enough, to help monitor what I was eating to make sure I did not exceed my daily allotment, it was a group effort to get me where I am today.

Long before I had carried the cross also, it was my mother, my father, and my family. The cross was heavy, as if it were made of stone. Yet we persevered, we managed. The weight never seemed to lessen. There were many occasions when no one knew, especially the medical community, if the treatment they were placing on would work.

The doctors refused to recommend the path that we chose, but it was the only option.

For the alternative, due to the buildup of toxins in my blood from eating foods which my liver could not process, would be devastating to my mind and central nervous system, causing significant damage to the brain itself, affecting judgement, coordination, mood, and much more. Additionally, with extreme mismanagement, there could be seizures.

I could have had a life of severe mental challenges to the point of needing daily assistance to live.

I could have had a life that led me to prison; and I could have had a life that led me to an early grave. No one would let me have that type of outcome.

Andrew must have a normal life. His mind must be protected. It was not an option to fail.

But how?

Everything was so new.

And uncertain.

And rare.

Yet the challenges of mismanagement were not what had happened, despite the challenges; for the angels were destined to visit me, and long before I was aware that I was different. Has my life been truly normal?

The influences of destiny wrapped their wings around me with the determination of those in my life to protect my brain as it developed, and their protection continues to this day, as each day is a day to manage the condition which, if mismanaged, constantly threatens to change everything.

My mind may have developed on its own in an extraordinary way with unique results; no one knew, when I was born, that I was destined to become an award-winning author. Yet, still, as I write this, the three letters follow me, day to day, throughout time, and on my journey, claiming to have the upper hand in my life.

Despite the success I have experienced, they still haunt me.

We are the weight of the cross, Andrew. We are the obstacles in your journey. And we will always be your destiny.

But I was never destined to have those three letters limit my potential of what I *could become*, which the angels in my life reminded me. The three letters are the shadows which have followed me and always threatened to darken my life; they were always there.

I would always carry them; they would continue to follow me, from my first step to my last.

And sometimes, they might feel like they are winning. Even now, at times. They reach for me; always follow me and still do.

Like shadows.

They would become part of me, but I refused to let them define me. Despite my initial concealing of any aspect of my personality or eating habits from others for fear of being ostracized for being different, to my more recent embracing of everything unique about me, in the beginning, my destiny was far less certain.

Could I have the courage to accept my being different from others?

Andrew had to have normal brain development. It was not an option to fail.

That was the decision my parents made, my mother and my father, together. Andrew would not live a completely normal life due to the condition, but the mind had to be protected. A lifetime of required assistance would not have been appealing if it could be avoided.

There was a glimmer of hope.

As one of the first babies to be placed on a treatment plan, which consisted of diet and strict blood monitoring, the hope penetrated an otherwise dark cloud which carried itself over my beginning in this earthly realm.

The doctors wouldn't recommend the treatment because it was so new; it was an experiment. But that was the catalyst. My parents knew that it was the thread which a possible positive outcome hung upon.

My birth was life-changing to them; although they were aware of the condition Phenylketonuria, known as PKU in the medical community and among the few families who had afflicted members, my parents knew little about PKU, and when I was born into the world, they took the first step in their journey.

But despite the uncertainties, my mind was preserved, with the intervention of my mother and father, and my siblings, and my doctors.

The world, as it was known then, knew little – and honestly, nothing at best – about the conditions with which I was afflicted and still am. The world carried on and still does, and although my condition is rare – a mere one in twenty thousand people have it – it has become a defining purpose in my life and the lives of others.

Could it have led to my anxieties, in particular? Did it contribute to the hypochondria I suffered from during periods of my adult life?

Or my test anxiety?

During my childhood and adolescence, I was subject to consistent and regular blood test monitoring to determine the course of my treatment, and if the diet and supplementary formulas were giving my body the nutrition it needed, but also to regulate my protein intake to ensure that it did not exceed safe levels in my bloodstream, which could have disastrous effects.

Throughout my life, from when I was a young boy to now as a middle-aged man, I have always held a deep fascination with the unknown, and, sometimes, it could be why I find my own story fascinating. When I was born, I was the epitome of the unknown. Despite that, I was blissfully unaware that there could be anything different than what I was experiencing. Yet my family experienced the uncertainty then. I

In those days, my parents carried the cross, as my brother was a toddler, and my sister was yet to be born. But my siblings were also destined to become part of the journey.

Quite significantly so.

There is something about the purpose of family.

They are those people who trust each other the most; and whether the family is biological or chosen, there are those who are brought together through birth. Parents find each other, those who were always meant to find each other, whether they knew it or not when meeting each other for the first time.

They were meant to bring their children into the world, all as connected souls. My parents were destined to meet, and bring me, and my siblings, into the world. I don't know if my siblings were different people if my successful outcome would be the same.

The path that was laid out before me was one that I could not forage alone.

Those who have been closest to me have been the angels of protection which I have needed; theirs were the voices in my head, which still speak to me silently to this day, warning me not to eat something that I would regret later. As my mind developed, although I did not see, or understand, what was transpiring with my sense of intuition, I now look back and realize.

My mind, as it may be, remains deeply connected to the things we are unable to see, or fully understand, or even prove. Perhaps that is where my love for the universe, particularly from a supernatural perspective, originated from; however, as I better understand how my mind developed, I see that there was much influence in my life, to ensure that my mind developed in the best way that it could. This ensured that I received the best nutrition I could, avoided what my body was unable to process, and lived as normal of a childhood as possible.

There are also those who have passed on whose voices of the past remain with me, as I better understand their contributions as well. They all remain in my life, whispering ancestral encouragement, to guide me through the journey as the development of my mind. The many ghosts, along with those still living, were the angels who made sure that there was something for me to eat when we entered a restaurant, or an event, or a gathering which was like stepping into the unknown.

Although the path which lay before me did not start to reveal itself to me until later in life, others who knew me as a child knew that I would have a special journey. There was something about Andrew, they said. He is destined to do something special, they said again. There was a specific purpose for me, others would say as I was a child.

There is something about Andrew.

And those three letters. Yet, I had the cross that I was called to carry.

My mother initially picked it up – carrying it when I was a mere infant, and my father was travelling to support the family. When she argued with doctors that she wanted to breast feed me for the proper formation of my mind, despite the warnings from the medical community that breast feeding would not work for a baby with my condition. I need special formulas, they said. If you breast feed him, his mind will not develop properly, they reminded my parents. He will live a life of being mentally challenged and requiring assistance, they repeated.

But that is the honest truth.

Many foods become toxic to me as I cannot break them down properly, and it seemed that I was destined to be a *retard* as some of the school children would tease when I was in elementary school. "You're a fricken' *retard* man. Your house is hot, and it *smells*. I only stayed there because my mom *made* me."

I wasn't quite sure then why I didn't fit in with the others, but now, I completely understand it.

I was different. There was just something about *Andrew*.

Always has been, always will be.

My unique personality and characteristics didn't keep me in those days from trying to connect with others when I was a boy – with my classmates, and the neighbors – and I did make some friends. Some were true friends, others, as I look back, only were my friends when they were just the two of us. But I do know that people, generally, and throughout my life, have been fascinated with me in one form or another.

It's like my fascination with the unknown.

When I was a child, I had no idea I was any different than anyone else other than the way I ate.

I didn't always understand why I ate the way I did, but I wasn't carrying the cross in those days. I just continued to stare, and wonder, and listen to the world. There was something there for me, it seemed.

A purpose.

Something was calling me. And then, I knew that despite the cross, despite the differences, I was made that way because the path laid for me to follow was one which other people might aspire to.

But often, the path was shrouded in darkness.

There would be uncertainty which would wash through me; the anxiety would set in as I would wonder what the outcome of a situation might be.

Yet when I was a child, I didn't know that I had anxiety. Or that my PKU could be contributing to it.

Because the anxiety simply was, is, and probably will always be a side effect; the PKU disorder didn't always cause my panic when it was mismanaged. It was managed quite well when I was a child. Yet despite that, the PKU has contributed to deep anxiety even when the diet is managed properly. Because even when the diet is followed as instructed – everything eaten must be measured exactly, counted, and written down in a list which the dietician would review during bi-annual specialist visits, things can happen.

Because that is how the world works.

Oh, that juice had an artificial sweetener? Well, of course, there goes the diet.

Oh, was there cheese in that recipe?

There goes the diet, yet again.

The symptoms of a PKU diet being mismanaged, even if unintentionally, come like a thief in the night. The skin does not break out; the throat does not close up. I would feel just fine. But later, maybe hours, maybe a day, perhaps two days...it would start.

I might become irritable and angry with the world. Or be unable to focus. Or my skin would erupt.

L

I knew my grandma, my mother's mother, was a "worry wart" as we lovingly called her.

I remember nights when I was commuting to college and still living at home, she would pace in the house, in the throes of the ravages of Alzheimer's disease, wanting to go home, back to her life she knew, away from the uncertainty of the time she was living, and back to the comfort of the past.

"I want to go home," she would tell my mother.

I was still young but no longer a child in those days, when my grandmother was living with us. Back then, I couldn't see the pain on my mother's face as my grandmother would repeat the phrase, over and over. She was already in her eighties, and my mother had moved her to our house to live as we were concerned for her safety living across the country alone at her age, and especially with a condition like Alzheimer's. The nightly ritual continued, and I watched, as my mother, with a tired look on her face, continued to clean the kitchen as I loaded the dishwasher, placing each dish inside as quietly and delicately as I could.

My grandmother would sit on a small stool at the counter opposite the sink, watching my mother rinse the dishes and place them in the dishwasher. She would look at my mother, her eyes wide, her face shifted, her lips pursed.

There was a sound of defeat in my mother's voice, yet still with love, and exhaustion. "You live here now, mom. Your room is down the hallway." I raised my head as I eased the plate in the dishwasher; delicately, scarcely making a sound. I looked over at my grandma, and her eyes were wide, and she shifted her gaze around the kitchen, pleading. She would sit on the stool across from the sink and stare at my mother intensely. "You can't keep me here," grandma said. "*I need to go home. I have things I need to take care of there. You can't keep me here.*"

My mother stopped cleaning the kitchen and walked over to her mother. She placed her arms around her and placed her head on her shoulder. "Mom," her voice cracked, as he placed her hand on the back of Grandma's head. "I wish you could, mom. I really wish I could."

I turned around slowly. "Goodnight, mom." I called over to her softly, knowing that there was nothing she could do, nor I.

She slowly raised her head, as my Grandma buried her head into my mother's shoulder, crying, asking her to bring her home. My mother looked up at me with tears streaming down her face. "Good night, Andrew. Thanks for helping."

I watched my mother comfort her own mother from the distance in the foyer, looking for a moment into the kitchen, as my grandma, wrapped my mother's loving embrace, as they hugged tightly.

L

A few years prior to that night, my mother and I made the trip several states away to assist my grandmother at her apartment, and drive her car, a 1986 Pontiac Grand Am, lime green complete with rusted tire wells, the nearly one-thousand-mile journey home back to the East coast. I was a new driver at the time, and with college around the corner, I would need a car. And Grandma's Pontiac was the best option.

It sat near her apartment, unused. When she did use it, there was a clear concern for her safety and the safety of others.

And there was worry and concern that she shouldn't be driving anyway. So my mother decided that it would solve two problems: her mother would no longer have a car to drive, which she did not need anyway, and she could rest easier, temporarily, knowing that her mother wasn't a thousand miles away, driving around in a car, when she shouldn't be.

And her son, me, would have a car to commute to college the following year.

While everyone in the family agreed that I needed to have a college experience of living somewhat on my own and away from the protection of the family nest, no one had a readily available solution to figure out how to effectively manage my PKU without the support of my family and medical team.

At that point, my high school years had already proven to be a struggle with maintaining the diet, and although I was accepted to an accredited private university in Philadelphia, we all thought it best for me to stay home initially and commute to school, although the drive was a full hour each way, to ensure that my diet and PKU treatment wouldn't derail.

As I sat in the kitchen on the small wooden stool at the counter, looking at my mother, and the man she was dating exclusively, I felt the anxiety creep through me.

I wondered what would come next for me, as I was about to embark on a new chapter in my life. It was this man, who had become another father figure in my life at that point, after my parents' divorce years earlier, who had helped guide me through that process. He and I sat, discussing my new acceptance to the university, and plans for the upcoming years.

"We agree that every young man, like yourself, needs to have the college experience, Andrew," he said.

I could feel my heart race in my chest in my attempt to maintain my composure.

How would I manage my PKU diet on a college campus? When I was a senior in high school, I had then recently emerged from several years of cheating on the diet, but in college, there would be many new experiences, and people, and pressure, and many different foods. All that would come towards me, without the watchful eye of my family.

How would I get my blood levels checked?

At home, in my own peaceful little world, we found a solution to the horrific lancets which my mother would have to stab my finger with. "We have to check your blood levels, Andrew," I would be told. "We have to make sure that you are not taking in too much protein. For when the symptoms come, damage has already been done."

I was set up for a blood draw in my arm, which, to me, was far less painful, although it required a weekly trip to my doctor's office. And several days of anxious waiting for the test results. For I knew, the blood test results always revealed how I'd been eating that week.

"We can figure all that out, Andrew," he said. "Don't worry. You worry too much!"

And then I would think back to the night when my grandmother was in the kitchen, wanting to go home. In her mind she needed to go somewhere else, but in actuality, she was already home. It's interesting how the mind works, and how it can so easily betray us. The old saying goes that ignorance is bliss, yet is it really? Thoughts can be willed into action, but things can still happen, even if one chooses to bury their head in the sand and pretend that the world isn't falling down around them.

As I went into my room, I drew up the shade, looking out in the night sky, and up towards the moon. In those days, I cast my gaze upwards in the same fashion I do now, then without realizing the meaning, and the significance, of looking into the cosmos.

Now, when I stare at the night sky, I think of the journey.

I look up at the stars, like sentinels keeping watch over the planets. Tiny, white pinpoints in a darkened sky; visible and watchable, watching us watching them. We can see what appears to be a twinkle.

And as we live in our minds, our thoughts cast to a mysterious beach on the cosmic shores, we stand, looking upwards to the unknown, gazing and wondering, what may be, what may reside beyond this planet, this place we have spent our every existence on. Later we learn that the twinkle was the passage of a distant planet, one which we would never be able to reach in our lifetime, in a world so far that we may never be able to fathom what could be there.

The star twinkles but for a moment; that point in time is a mere fragment of existence, yet circumstantial when considered beyond. There's a saying that a lifetime on Earth can be a heartbeat in Heaven; and it's the stars that guide us towards that notion. The steady, twinkling beacons which are always there standing command over us, bring destiny. The twinkle, the tiny flash, happens. Fleeting moments; discreet opportunities, yearning for movement forward on the journey.

And then the star shines steadily once again.

When I walk at night, and stand in the moonlight, I feel a spiritual connectedness to other worlds which seem distant from what is practical and what is physical. But, in my mind, I now know that everything is connected. I think about those souls we know, and might want to, who have soared into the cosmos before us. The spirits who have taken journeys toward distant realms; through the interstellar; to other worlds, and different planes, like the stardust, of which we are all made, continue its shower outwards. Raining

45

on other galaxies which humanity may never be able to explore within the confinement of a physical human life.

It would be as if I'd left my body lying on a beach with delicate lapping waters, on the shores below, as me – who I was, and what was truly *me* – soared upwards as I imagined the planets in our solar system, and beyond, and wonder what it would be like if I could soar across the universe as if I were a soul. Drifting forward at speeds incomprehensible and unimaginable. Flying on a journey which would promise to captivate me, to inspire me, and to grasp me in its ferocious pastel butterflies and nebulae; its planets which I had yearned to see and wanted to explore; its comets; the Pillars of Creation; the undeniable beauty of the cosmos.

I knew that science would gently whisper in my ear at one point, but not when I expected it to.

A number of years were destined to pass after my childhood when I took a more practical direction in my early adult life as opposed to my current calling to the artistic and spiritual.

Although, as a child, I found my middle school Earth science classes interesting, and my paper mâché volcano, which I painstakingly crafted on one of our small, round plastic kitchen plates that my mother graciously agreed to sacrifice for creativity, thrilled my classmates, as I combined the baking soda, vinegar, and red food coloring to make my volcano "erupt".

The students clapped as my teacher congratulated me for having such a well-constructed volcano. And she was right, I thought. My brother had helped me in the days prior, who was also excited about science, after reading books by opening them so discreetly that the spine would not wrinkle. And he was always known to have the best-preserved books on the block. He was a lover of science; he was and still is.

"Come on, Andrew," my brother said, as he dredged a strip of newspaper in the mixture of flour and water. He gingerly added the strip to the forming mountain as I continued tearing strips from the old papers. The mountain was being created on an old, white plastic plate which became some of our go-to plates. We had saved them from old TV dinners, and despite them being small, they were the perfect size for us. Although one was being sacrificed, my brother helped me dip the strips of newspaper in the flour and water mixture, as we layered them together, strip after strip, until the mountain formed.

"Now we have to let it dry and set," he said. We placed it in the garage until the next day, when we sat at the kitchen table again, with the small mountain;

it looked dry and crusty white with mussed newsprint. "Let's paint it grey!"

I clapped, excited as my love of science began.

CHAPTER TWO

Before she passed away, my aunt was my pen pal.

It was during those early years, when I was still a child, before I was in high school, which the letters had wrapped around me like a security blanket.

Those years when the letters came, I had always known her; she was my mother's sister. It was after the days when my family and I would fly from the east coast to the west coast of the United States, where she lived a great deal of her life; she and I remained connected as I grew.

Now, as I write this, I feel that she is a kindred spirit, the kind who taught me to look beyond the surface. Upwards and outwards, towards the unknown, and always into uncharted waters and across the mysteriousness of the universe.

We used to write letters to one another, and I would run back inside the house from the mailbox, giddy and skipping, holding the letter in my hand. When I arrived in the kitchen, I flopped my backpack into a chair and examined the envelope.

There was her handwriting.

Familiar, fun, with exaggerated looping letters; something I had always looked forward to. The days when I received the letters in the mail were greatly anticipated, for I knew she would respond to my questions, my theories, and my thoughts that only a little boy could concoct.

The letters, though, were not about cars, cartoons, or even school subjects.

My thoughts may have been different for a boy younger than ten, but my aunt replied to my letters, every single one, and I was excited to read them, and then reply.

In those days, we wrote letters back and forth to one another about more practical and Earthly subjects. My mind was forming, my family was ensuring that despite the hurdles we constantly had to face, regardless of the odds of success which worked against us presented themselves.

But my family all actively worked to preserve my mind for that destiny which it was meant for.

While my aunt and I wrote letters which discussed just about anything and everything, we had not yet touched on the mysteriousness of the cosmos and our shared passion for outer space.

"You are out of this world!" my mother said as she dressed me in a small, yellow T-shirt with a cosmic scene printed on the front which gave a source to her words. *Out of this world*, the lettering read; the text was streamed at the bottom of the cosmic scene, and it was perfect for a little boy who was destined to have a fascination of what lies beyond, whether it be another realm, or a distant galaxy.

The letters with my aunt that stuck out in my mind, and the letters that I remember the most, were when we were going back and forth about Las Vegas and Atlantic City.

I'm not much of a gambler, she wrote. *But your uncle has his trade shows here for the car parts, and I know he likes to play craps, but I honestly just like to read my book. We usually stay at the Las Vegas Hilton, and I sit on a bench outside of the casino and read my book.*

She knew I liked to collect the slot machine coin gathering plastic cups; I had several of them from Atlantic City, from when my mother would run into the casino to get for one me, because I was still too young to enter.

It was when we gathered those coin cups, with the casino hotel logos on the side, we went to the Sands Hotel and Casino near the Boardwalk in Atlantic City, so my mother could attend the PKU conference, to learn more about new developments for the condition I was born with.

I remember going to the conferences with her, and it was an annual day of fun that I looked forward to. I was still a child, but I loved heading to the excitement of Atlantic City. I remember sitting at the classroom tables in one of the smaller ballrooms at the Sands, and I would go and collect the complimentary pads and pens from the tables after the sessions were over, shoving them into my plastic bag.

The staff looked at me yet said nothing; although years later, when I was a Banquet Manager, I understood the cost of those items, and also the thoughts that may have been entering the minds of the banquet staff at the Sands, as they watched a young boy shove all of their pads and pens into his small, plastic bag.

I enjoyed the food break set on small tables in the back of the room, all made specially with PKU foods, so me, and the other children like me, could eat freely while their parents listened to the doctors. My mother sat ahead at the table, taking notes, listening to the speakers intently, one of which was my doctor. Other dieticians and clinical staff were discussing the innovations of the treatment of Phenylketonuria.

But this was the 1980's.

The foods that I enjoyed on the back table had a long way to go in taste and texture. They were special breads at the time, because bread had protein. And it was protein that my liver could not break down. I was limited mostly to fruits and vegetables, but everything had to be counted and measured.

At the Sands, I had never seen my special bread look so fancy and appealing; cut meticulously, and arranged on plates in pinwheels, with assorted jams and jellies and fruits. Seeing that arrangement of my diet foods made me feel special.

Like I belonged.

I was excited to eat them; all of the children there were eating them, as were the adults and others. It became normal, and that was encouraging. The foods were presented exquisitely with the other foods, and small slices of colorful fruits arranged artistically on large plates. For everyone at the conference was eating PKU foods.

Not just me.

And that may have been where the excitement of attending this annual conference originated from.

In that ballroom, everyone was eating the food that I was eating. No matter how "off" they may have looked or tasted. And there were only a few in that ballroom who had the condition, as most were family members, like my mother, who were seeking new treatments. And the others were medical staff and researchers.

But everyone ate the food.

And then, I felt normal.

But then, was I really all that different?

People throughout the world also suffer from their own afflictions. What made my condition any different than all the others?

As I sit and write this, and recall, and think, and remember, I think about all the other conditions that people have. I know so much about other conditions, like Diabetes, and Crohn's Disease. Even

Neurofibromatosis. So many, too many to keep track of, unless one is forced to understand.

Few people know about Phenylketonuria.

I may have had a cross to carry, but we all have. I may have had challenges and setbacks throughout my life, but we all have them. And I have also had my gifts, which we all have as well.

As with many others, it took years, and the influence of other people, to help my discovery of where within myself my talent would be, and how I could discover it, and develop and nurture it, and share it with the world. But most importantly…what my talent was in my mind.

And so, I am taking this opportunity to share my story with everyone, which has been an extraordinary journey for me.

At the time of this writing, this book has already been in the writing process, at some stage or another, for nearly two decades. I knew that *Three Letters* was always a story that I wanted to tell. I felt compelled to tell it, but now looking back, I believe that I needed to find the courage to face a lot of what is discussed in this book.

Could my anxiety be the result of the PKU diet?

I learned, while writing this book, that Generalized Anxiety Disorder (GAD) is an inherited condition that many people have. I know that my maternal grandmother had it, or at least some form of it, before she became afflicted with Alzheimer's Disease later in her life. What I did not know, at least as a child, is that I didn't always understand the correlation between Phenylketonuria and GAD.

When writing this book, I better understood the connection between the two conditions and how, sometimes when I would be "a little too relaxed" with managing my PKU, I could be my own worst enemy.

I don't actively cheat on the diet as an adult, as I understand that potential ramifications. But now, as a middle-aged man, I could, theoretically, liberalize the diet if I chose to on my own.

Most of the time, there's no one standing by my side, reminding me to watch what I am eating more carefully. No one is telling me to keep measuring my foods, or to write them down on a list so I remember what I had and do not overeat, because it is easy to lose track during the course of a day, when one is not actively tracking the food consumed.

It is my responsibility now.

As a young boy, I loved to receive those letters in the mail from my aunt in California.

I would run to the mailbox, yanking the small, rounded metal door of the box out towards me, and there were two things that I was looking for.

I peered inside, looking into the darkness through the circulars and envelopes which caught the daylight. They were bright white rectangles; those didn't matter to me unless I saw the familiar handwriting.

They filled the small black box.

I dug my hands inside, searching for the small, square brown box of my compact discs from the music service companies by mail that no one ever seemed to pay. And, naturally, also for letters from my aunt.

It was the letters that started my journey. There were many more than three, but I know that they were cherished and anticipated. My aunt and I, living on opposite coasts, had a connection with a depth that, when looking back, seemed rare for those separated by generations.

We discussed adult topics, such as outer space, and the cosmos. And more cosmopolitan things, like which was better: Atlantic City or Las Vegas.

Whenever I brought it up at church, I would ask the older ladies who would head to the casino city by the sea by bus on the weekends, which of the casino cities that they preferred. In those days, before the proliferation of gambling across many areas of the country, and online gambling, it was those two cities that were in direct competition, and there was little, if any, alternatives in other states.

Although the ladies visited Atlantic City religiously by bus to play the slot machines on a regular basis, they would always tell me, "Oh Las Vegas, of course. Atlantic City needs to add something besides casinos. Las Vegas has such a bigger advantage over A.C."

My shoulders would slump, and my head would tilt to the side as I heard them say that.

My mother and I had already been visiting the Sands in Atlantic City annually at that point, and I started to warm up to the city. I found it exciting going there, despite not being old enough to set foot inside a casino, and it became part of my life in a larger way once I headed to college.

The letters, though, back and forth with my aunt, continued over time, and I learned how much she was an avid reader.

I was astounded that my aunt, my mother's sister, could travel to a city like Las Vegas and lose herself in a book; the mysteriousness and excitement of a city like Las Vegas always appealed to me, and I would be destined to visit Sin City for the first time when I was in my twenties.

The exchange of letters with my aunt, and the Las Vegas casino cups she sent me (which I cherished) which she and my uncle mailed me, may have fueled my passion for Atlantic City.

It may be, at least partially, from the letters in those days, the passion which I still share, to a degree, to this day. It was an extra special day when they sent me a package with a stack of casino cups from the casinos along the strip, some of which have since closed at the time of the writing of this book, made me feel like I was a special boy.

With all of the glittering excitement of Las Vegas happening around her, my aunt chose to bury her nose in a book, tuning out the slot machine dings, boisterous wedding parties, loud drunks, and losing herself in a world of fiction, which, I learned, would become my own destiny. Later in life, she would be one of my biggest fans of the science fiction books I wrote.

"I don't much care for Andrew's supernatural thrillers," she had told my mother on a phone call a few years before she passed away. "But I really like his science fiction. I've been reading them, and I really enjoy them. He needs to keep writing them."

My aunt lived with my uncle and cousins in Southern California, and when we first went to visit them, I was a mere four years old. A ball of energy, loving life and everything about it. Ahead of our flight, my mother had called the airline to make sure there was something that I could eat on the plane, since we were flying from the east cost of the United States to California. And also, in the days when I was a small child, meal service was commonplace in domestic and also in coach class, and it became one of the reasons why I was so excited to fly on a plane for the first time.

My mother had called the airline before we left for the transcontinental flight to make sure there was something for me to eat on the plane. I couldn't have the normal fare – eggs, bacon, biscuits, and pancakes. "He can't have any of that," my mother said, as she cradled the phone on her shoulder.

She nodded, shifting the phone to the other ear, and looked over and down at me, and nodded, giving a thumbs up. "There's a lot of things Andrew can't have ma'am. We wouldn't be doing this unless we had to. If you are unable, we will figure something out."

"No, no," the airline representative said. "We are here to accommodate you, Mrs. Mengel. So, you have been explaining to me that Andrew cannot eat the eggs and bacon."

My mother switched the phone again from one shoulder to the other. "It's a lot more than that," she said. "Eggs, milk, there's a whole list."

"So, pancakes wouldn't work then?"

My mother lowered her head and closed her eyes. "It needs to be dairy free and as low in protein as it can be."

There was a brief pause. "May I place you on hold, Mrs. Mengel?"

My mother let out an exasperated sigh. "Sure, go ahead."

The hold music started playing, as my mother shifted the phone from one shoulder to the other, and stopped over the long, coiled cord to put some plates in the dishwasher.

After a few minutes, the woman came back on.

"We can make him some special crepes," she said. "The stewardesses also have some grape jelly, and they can roll them up for them."

My mother nodded slowly and lifted the cord up as my brother skipped through and under the cord as she held it. "Yes, yes, thank you for that accommodation," she said. "But I would like to see if we can all have that meal."

There was silence on the line for a few moments. My mother shifted the phone from one shoulder to the other.

"Hello?"

The voice crackled through the line. "Yes, yes, Mrs. Mengel. So, you are saying that you want four special meals?"

"Yes, that is what I am saying. It is important that my son receives what we are having. I don't want there to be any big fanfare. Let him see that he is eating exactly what we are eating."

After a moment, the woman's voice crackled through the line again. "Oh, I see, Mrs. Mengel. So, he is autistic?"

My mother sighed. "No, no. He isn't autistic. He has a condition called Phenylketonuria. We call it PKU for short."

"PK – what?"

"PKU. He is missing an enzyme in his liver and cannot process protein. If he eats too much of it, it builds up in his blood and becomes toxic to his body. It's okay, ma'am. There aren't many who know about this condition. And for our Andrew, he has to have a very strict special diet because his body can't process the protein, and it builds up in his bloodstream and can become toxic. Do you have children?"

There was another brief pause. "Yes, Mrs. Mengel. I have a son and a daughter."

And that is when the tide turned. As they spoke, my mother made a connection with a representative from the airline's customer service department, in the time when meals were commonplace on airlines, because she took the time to help someone understand. PKU goes far beyond one family doing what is best for their own son, it was about what all families do for all of our children. We

63

want what is best for them and overall, we want them to be happy. We want them to be happy, and to feel loved, and to feel like they belong.

And this is what happened on my first flight.

When the flight attendant placed my tray in front of me, with the two crepes rolled up in grape jelly, I looked over at what my mother, father and brother had, and they had the same thing. I was overjoyed, jumped in my seat and clapped, laughing and giggling. Now, decades later, I understand how I felt. My food was the same as everyone else's. It was not different; it was not weird or special. I didn't notice that the other people on the plane were getting the eggs and bacon which my family would have normally been getting.

They were all happy with their crepes rolled in grape jelly, and I felt included. It was in the years when I was on a quest to be the same as everyone else, I had yet to realize the beauty of being different and unique.

But in those days, when we all ate our rolled crepes in grape jelly, on the plane which was the first flight I ever took, to my aunt's house in California, who was destined to be a pen pal within the coming years, was when the angels in my family had banded together to make sure that Andrew would not feel excluded.

And for that, I felt special.

CHAPTER THREE

For the longest time, I worked hard to prevent the world from discovering that I was different.

Until I chose to embrace it.

And now, as an author, I work tirelessly to show the world that *I am different.* I want to be the new voice; the undiscovered talent that the world has been waiting for. I want to separate myself from others who have taken similar paths before me; I want to carve my own destiny from a different wood with a newly formed blade.

As I looked, the rust was forming at the ridges.

I plunged it into the tree, cursing myself. There were too many obstacles, it seemed. Could carving one's initials into a tree bring legacy? Was there a reason, or a purpose, for our existence and what we leave behind for the world to discover once we are gone?

We all seem to be somewhere in time.

And time can exist as a moment, in a cascade of moments, forming together as a journey, which we all share, and all experience, and all remember. Despite our differences, we are truly the same. We all stand on the same beach, looking outwards towards the horizon above the endless, infinite ocean.

And we all see the stones.

They are laid out before us, reaching outwards into the mystery and uncertainty of the sea, small, grey islands in swirling waters, crashing against them with spraying white foam. They stretch far beyond the horizon, beyond our own vision and what it allows us to see. The stones begin with the comfort and solace of the sands; the security of land and the knowledge which we will not drown. The next stone seems far, practically out of reach as the waves crash and spray seemingly angry white foam into the air.

Too far to jump, too slippery to stand.

But we humans are resourceful. We recognize problems and break them down until we understand them and find the help we need to move to that next stone and stand on our own two feet. We keep moving forward, despite our trepidation, for time disallows us to stand still. It will proceed, with or without us, and whether we choose to embrace the marriage between time and movement or not, it will drag us forward with it towards a destiny which we all hold the power to determine, or simply experience, despite the many setbacks and challenges which we all face.

It's a cliché to say that life is full of obstacles, but clichés are what they are for a reason. For every successful person, there is an era when that person was struggling. When the bills didn't always get paid, when the concealing fog refused to lift, despite looking upwards and seeing the sun fighting to burn it off. But that is when the stones are most intimidating; they remain wet with the mist and waters of the crashing waves.

But like that successful person, by looking within, the fortitude to remain standing through the crashing waves and uncertainty, purpose can be found.

Regardless of whether the journey, and the legacy, is through the creation of new generations to discover and explore and carry a name through the years and decades; or finding a legacy that could be left through something – a tangible *thing* – left for the world to discover, the thought of legacy really is no different. And finally, there are actions which earn us remembrance, both good and bad.

There are times when I wondered how to approach this book. It's a story of my life, yes, but the focus is really Phenylketonuria. It's PKU. My three letters that follow me around like the shadows they are. Like us all, I am interdimensional; I think and feel deeply, and I wonder, just as we all do, why I am here.

Why was I placed on the Earth simply to have the challenges?

And even more so, why was I given a metabolic disorder that would prove to be a cross to carry, a heavy burden to bear, not only for myself, but for my parents, and my family, and anyone else who becomes deeply involved in my life? Why was that my chosen destiny?

There were so many seemingly unanswerable questions.

We exist.

Even after death.

Yet before we were born into this world, before humans walked the earth, as the Universe was created, there was a shower of carbon and stardust which rained on our planet, and together with water, provided the necessary ingredients to form life. Many know that the most basic forms of life evolved into who we are as people today; but that did not happen without the nourishment of every life form's most basic needs.

Throughout generations, there have been differences in interpretation of the creation of the Universe; of what it was.

But it remains one of the greatest mysteries; the destiny of the cosmos brings life, and its subsequent fragility to our consciousness.

While we are living, we may never know for certain whether the formation of the Universe was the result of a series of reactions or initiated by the hand of a supreme being. Yet the mystery of humanity is shared by all; none of us *truly* know what will happen when we close our eyes for the last time. Although we do share the same aspirations as human beings – we all want to be remembered, in one form or another.

And once we are born and enter the world from the warmth and comfort of the womb, we need.

Suddenly in this big, cold, scary world which we were thrust into. From the moment of our birth, we start to need. And our needs, should they not be fulfilled, have the potential to send us to the grave; not only as an individual who had lived and loved and experienced for decades, but also as a newly born infant. Should the needs of the *baby* not be addressed, that new child can leave this world nearly as fast – or possibly much faster – than entered.

The excitement or the anxiety of the pregnancy announcement has been experienced by many families, if not all, throughout the world, regardless of country of origin, or religious or political affiliation, or ethnicity or age. The news of a baby coming into the family can be exciting; it's a continuation of the journey. Of the family name. Of the legacy of the ancestors.

One of the reasons why we are here.

A new soul is preparing to enter the world; a baby is being formed, humans have come together to create. It's one of the gifts we have been afforded and all share. Just as the needs we all require.

Food, water, shelter, love.

The four basic needs, in essence, are few, but paramount to survival.

And we all have them, no matter what we are destined to achieve in this world, no matter what our legacy may be. The basic needs of survival are the same for the serial killer as they are for the Nobel Prize winner.

And they are the same for me, as they are for you.

We all have many different needs; there may be some who believe we need spirituality, or soul nourishment in one form or another. But there are many who exist in the physical world and do not recognize other realms of existence.

And they survive just fine.

I do know my mother, a devout Catholic, would not survive if she did not have her need of faith fulfilled. And still, I know others who do not understand, or need, that type of living doctrine to flourish.

But the basic needs – the physical requirements to sustain life – are the same for every human being living on this planet.

Food, water, shelter, love.

The world in the early twenty-first century is vastly different than it was when I was a child in the 1980's. Back then, I had blonde hair cut in a bowl over my head, from which I would soon snip a perfect square from my bangs in first grade the night before school picture day with a pair of scissors I found. I slowly got down from the stool and walked into the kitchen, scissors still in hand. "Look mom! I gave myself a haircut!"

Her eyes widened and her mouth dropped open.

She covered her mouth with her hand, and reached down, taking the scissors and placing them on a high shelf I could not access. "Your first-grade school pictures are tomorrow, Andrew! We can't have a picture of you with a square cut out of your bangs!"

I have memories of my mother, trying to comb my hair forward easing the bangs together, in an attempt to cover the square, in desperation. The images floated through my mind, but the resulting photo told a different story: that the camera does not lie. It showed that I decided to moonlight as a barber, at least for one evening. The photo always reminds me of that day.

In essence, however, I was a normal boy. Inquisitive, and filled with wonder and curiosity. I was interested in cars, and in music, and in superheroes.

Physically, I was small, always smaller than my classmates and friends, to my own dismay. Now, I as a man, I am still small. I have learned to respect my body, knowing that I will always be able to connect my thumb and forefinger if I circle them around my wrist.

"It's a result of the PKU," the doctor had told my mother in one of my routine checkups when I was still a young child. My mind seemed to wander as I glanced around the room, looking at the hanging posters with health recommendations set against the stark white walls. I saw the small, triangular rubber hammer lying on the nearby counter as my mother talked with the doctor. I never rendered much concern to these appointments, just more inquisitiveness.

I grabbed the shiny, slim handle and picked up the small, rubber mallet, using my other hand to touch the chrome. The doctor leaned forward and reached for the instrument. "Let's check your reflexes, Andrew."

I sat on the bed, crinkling the thin, white paper with my fingers on either side of my hips. The doctor tapped the mallet on my knee, sending a slight buzz into my body as my leg flung forward toward his billowing white coat. "Very good, Andrew. You have good reflexes. Now let's check your other knee."

I grinned, tightening my leg.

He tapped my knee, and I concentrated on holding my leg still. His forehead crinkled and he lightly tapped again. I shot my leg up, whooshing his coat behind him. My mother looked up from the small, plastic chair on the other side of the exam room as the doctor chuckled, placing the mallet on the side counter.

"Well, Andrew, you are quite the showman indeed." He washed his hands in a small sink, and as he tore a paper towel from the side dispenser, he turned to face my mother. "His reflexes are fine. And the levels have been in the acceptable range. We need to keep a close eye on them for another year or so. We may be able to take him off diet then."

My mother tilted her head to the side. "I don't understand…off the diet?"

I watched as the doctor leaned against the counter, folding his arms. "Of course," he said. "You know the brain is almost fully developed. And Andrew's PKU only affects the brain when it is developing. He should be able to be taken off diet soon."

My mother drew her breath in, slowly shaking her head. "I don't know, doctor. Everything has been working. I don't know if we should take him off of the diet. How do we know that he won't digress?"

"Well, there is still a lot that we are learning about this metabolic condition."

Her eyes fell and she looked down into her lap, shuffling some papers. "Then how do we know that the diet is only needed during the initial years? I don't think we should take him off his diet." She held up the small stack of paperwork. "I have read some of the journals myself," she said. "The years of brain development are under debate. I work with the developmentally disabled. I know of some of the mentally challenged people that lived with undiagnosed PKU, and they need everything taken care of for them. *Everything.* They can't do anything for themselves. And Andrew has been doing so well. Why would we even *consider* taking him off the diet?"

The doctor nodded as he jotted some notes in the manila folder. "Of course, Andrew is your son," he said, not looking up as he scribbled. "The decision, naturally, is yours."

My mother held my coat out for me as I slid into the arms.

"The diet seems to be working," she said, zipping me up. "I think we should keep him on the diet. I've seen too many people whose untreated PKU have made them unable to live normal *lives*, doctor."

The doctor nodded. "Mrs. Mengel, yes. I am aware of the effects of PKU on the mind and central nervous system."

"And of course we know what could happen to Andrew if his blood levels rise to unsafe levels."

"Severe brain disorders," the doctor said. "Nervous system impairment. Even irreversible damage. Mental impedance, of course. We have seen that in the past. Before we had this treatment, of course."

"Which no one would recommend in Dayton when Andrew was an infant."

"We are starting to understand PKU a little better now, Mrs. Mengel. Andrew's blood phenylalanine levels have been within range, and now, you can liberalize the diet. If you choose."

My mother shook her head. She stared at the doctor directly. "You didn't know much at all when Andrew was born. And do you really know much more now?"

"There's a study saying that we can take children off of the restrictive diet around age six."

She folded her arms. "Andrew is going to stay on the diet."

Despite the doctors believing I could be able to be taken off of the diet, I remained on it, and I still adhere to the diet to this day.

Although I desperately wanted to put the diet behind me when I was a child, and those feelings continued throughout my adult life, even as I write this now.

The diet is not an easy one.

Not only for a child and the feelings of being different from the other children due to being required to eat specially prepared foods that the others did *not* eat, but also for an adult, when convenience foods have become the norm in an increasingly demanding society.

There have been those who have told me that the PKU diet is one of the most difficult and challenging to follow and manage. And there were always studies seeking to liberalize the diet, finding new and innovative ways to treat it, and mostly, to better understand the condition. But my mother's intuition was solid. A few years after we sat in the office with the doctor, another study came out, insisting that PKU parents put their children back on strict diets right away.

But by that time, the damage had already been done.

ℒ℈

The feelings of being different, somehow special, where each meal became a question of how much protein content was inside it, remained.

"You can't eat *protein*?!" people would ask me, all the time throughout my life. They found it difficult to understand that I could not eat meat. Or cheese; any type of dairy for that matter. Or any animal product.

"So, you're lactose intolerant?" they would ask me as a follow up question.

"No, no," I would say. "It's much more complicated than that."

"So, you are a vegetarian?"

I would nod. They were starting to understand. "In a way, yes."

Their faces would shift a bit. "What do you mean, in a way?"

"I cannot eat animal products."

Their eyes would light up as if they had an epiphany. "Ah ha!" They would always say something indicating they thought they had it all figured out. "So, you are a vegan! That's really becoming trendy these days. Wow, hats off to you!"

I would always chuckle a bit. "Well, it's a bit like that, but not exactly. I can't eat a lot of the high protein things vegans eat, like quinoa and beans."

I would get a confused stare. "How do you *survive*?!"

"My body still needs protein, just like yours. But I am missing the enzyme in my liver needed to break it down. You can even see it on the chart when

79

a doctor does my bloodwork. The protein enzyme for the liver tests always shows up as zero."

"That's unbelievable, I've never heard of that."

"It's pretty rare. Not too many people know much about it. But I do get some protein. I have a daily allotment that my body can tolerate, and I am not supposed to exceed that."

They would look at me, nodding as if they knew.

"I have Diabetes," they would offer. Or maybe it would be some other ailment.

And so, I understood. "So, you know, you have to track everything as well."

They had a cross to bear also.

We all have conditions that we deal with. None of us will be physically perfect, and any expectation of that would be unrealistic.

"It actually is kind of like Diabetes," I would respond. "My body still needs protein to survive and grow. I would be a complete mess and have quite a lot of deficiencies if I simply avoided protein altogether."

People usually want clarification. "But you can't eat it. What do you do?"

"I have to drink it," I would answer. "I drink a medically prescribed formula to get my protein already in a broken-down format. But I have a daily allotment which my body can tolerate, since protein is in most foods, just at different levels."

I have grown used to the line of questioning, as the questions continue to be the same. No matter what condition the asker has, whether it be Diabetes, IBS, Crohn's Disease, and others.

We have only been screening PKU since the early 1970's.

Dr. Robert Guthrie developed a test which changed public health. Although the disease is incredibly rare, with less than 300 infants born with the condition in the United States, it was found to be prudent to screen every baby shortly after birth.

I was screened, and I tested positive for the genetic condition.

In PubMed Journal, it was found that "for the diet to be effective…the otherwise normal-appearing infant with PKU must be identified, among thousands of unaffected infants, in the first weeks of life."

The test was made mandatory due to the threat to the development of the mind. There was speculation that individuals, prior to discovering the screening, who may have been committed to insane asylums, or in prisons, or in hospitals or group homes, with severely reduced mental acuity, could have been the result of untreated Phenylketonuria. It wasn't their fault; the condition simply had yet to be identified.

Treating PKU is like walking a tight rope.

There was always the threat that my mind would not develop properly, that I would not be able to live a normal life, that I would require assistance throughout my adult life. The protein isn't what is toxic to me. My body requires protein, just as yours does, to build strong bones and muscles, and to grow, and to be healthy. As my liver is missing the enzyme necessary to break down protein into the essential amino acids that our body requires, the result is phenylalanine, which builds up in my blood and becomes toxic to the brain and central nervous system.

The balance of the diet remains critical throughout life.

There are newer studies that speculate the human mind isn't fully developed until age twenty-five. In that case, my mind was still in a developmental stage during my high school years, which could be considered my "rebellious" years. And my rebellion wasn't in the traditional sense – it was simply against the diet and restrictions that were placed on my life, in my quest to fit in and be a *normal person.*

Had I done any damage to my mind during those years?

One could argue that I hadn't.

But could there be anything in my current adult life that could be considered a consequence of those years when I did not follow the required treatment as well as I should have?

In the subsequent years, I was accepted and attended a private university in Philadelphia. I maintained Dean's List grades for every semester, and I graduated Cum Laude with honors.

During that time, I was following my diet.

I stopped cheating, and my blood phenylalanine levels were in perfect range at every weekly blood test I had at the campus clinic. My mother would tell me that, since my blood levels were under control, I was finally making progress and living up to my potential. I remember answering her, saying that I still wanted to do something else.

I enjoyed myself during my college years and was meeting a lot of people and making a lot of friends, some of whom are still my friends to this day.

Yet there was something missing in my life.

I wasn't sure what it was. I considered my coursework, primarily in hospitality management and its related business, finance, and food production courses, but also my chosen electives of psychology, sociology, linguistics, and film studies. What direction was I taking unknowingly? Which stone on the journey was I on – or preparing for?

Only time would tell me, and it required me to open my mind to the many possibilities of where my life could lead me.

CHAPTER FOUR

I still remember watching the ball drop in my mother's living room, ushering in 1982 as the new year, long before the days when I started to discover the talent, and the creative fire, that was deep within me.

It was before the era of new forms of creative expression; long before the internet and computer graphics, I sat in my room, tracing an outline with a pencil from a cassette tape insert from a Prince tape, onto a piece of plain, white paper, drawing my artwork with my markers and crayons.

As I folded the paper to fit in the small plastic cassette tape box, now adorned with my own colorful artwork and inscribed with my name "Andi", I carefully placed it in the shiny plastic box and placed the tape inside, with dreams of a future as a pop star.

My mom entered, holding a laundry basket. "Andrew, do you have all of your school uniforms for next week?"

"I made a mix tape," I said, handing it to my mother. I looked up at her, noticing that she was still holding her bags from work. She looked tired, and then her face brightened.

She set her bags down slowly on the wooden stool next to the counter.

"Andrew," she said, turning the tape around in her hands, opening it up and taking it out. The same blue cassettes that we'd bought at K-mart the day before. "Why did you spell your name with an i?"

I folded my arms. "I am going to be a star," I said, with a note of confidence in my voice. "I need a name that everyone can know me by."

My mother smiled a tired smile and handed me the tape back. "I kind of like Andrew. That's what we named you."

"*I need a stage name.*"

"That's okay, you do you."

Despite the encouragement when I was a child, the uncertainty of my future hovered like a dark shadow for everyone in my life, except me.

It wasn't anything evil, it was simply unknown to me. There was much to me that simply seemed *normal* as I was growing up as a little boy.

A restrictive diet and frequent blood tests were all I knew. That was my version of normal. My parents were the ones who suffered from anxiety and uncertainty, for nothing was out of sorts from my perspective.

The old saying goes that ignorance is bliss, and for at least a portion of my life, I was blissfully unaware. I did not know of the challenges, the fear, and the wondering if my brain would develop normally.

For my simple existence was completely normal from my perspective.

This is just how life was, wasn't it?

It was normal – not different – to have special foods made for me, with low protein, because I was missing the liver enzyme to break down phenylalanine, which naturally occurs in food, to the essential amino acid tyrosine.

Yet my parents experienced a different journey.

The uncertainty and anxiety were very real to them.

"Your son has tested positive for Phenylketonuria," the doctor said, to my parents, shortly after I was born.

They sat across from him in the stark hospital room, as my mother cradled me in her arms, swaddling me in a blanket, watching as the doctor slid a chair closer to the bed. My mother's face shifted as she looked down at me, shaking her head.

She closed her eyes. "I know what that is."

My father sat down gently next to her on the bed, placing his arm around her.

The doctor cleared his throat. "Andrew is missing an enzyme in his liver, Mr. and Mrs. Mengel, and you have two choices at this point."

My father looked up. "And what are those?"

The doctor shifted in his chair as my father folded his arms, eyes piercing, as he stared at the doctor, searching for answers.

"The phenylalanine in his blood will build up and become toxic," the doctor said. "If he eats a normal diet. These are crucial, formative years for his brain. If he drinks breast milk, or baby formula, the phenylalanine will build up to toxic levels in his blood and he will suffer from brain disorders, will not fully develop, and will require assistance for his entire life. He may also be subject to seizures and tremors, as well as skin conditions."

My mother lowered her head to look down on me, giving me a kiss on my tiny head, as I slept in the blanket, held close to her chest in her arms. My father stood next to her, looking down at me, as my eyes were closed, and seemingly content.

She shook her head and looked up at my father.

My father turned to face the doctor. "But…what will Andrew eat? How will he survive? Or live, for that matter?"

As a newborn, I, of course, have no memories of that day.

It was not me that bore the cross in my early years, and it wasn't until I was an adolescent that the cross was handed to me to carry, but I've always had those near me to help me with the weight whenever I struggled. But the time I was born was the most interesting form of destiny that I could ever seem to have experienced, even now, as I write decades later, it seems unfathomable.

I sometimes wonder what type of destiny is meant for me when my parents got together, married, had three extraordinary children, then promptly divorced.

When exploring the mystery of angels, I have found that angels seem to run towards disaster and danger. They insert themselves in the most precarious of situations, and, if there are angels living in the world among us, which very well may be (and my mother firmly believes that there are) then the period we are living in would be the ideal period for angels to exist in the population.

PKU has never been an easy cross to bear, and it took the angels in my life to help; to ensure that my mind developed normally, for if I had been born a mere few years earlier, the diet and treatment which I was afforded had not yet been developed. And even so, when I was born, the treatment for PKU was so new that no one even knew if it would be effective.

"We don't know," the doctor said, when asking my parents' questions about whether the strict, low-protein diet would work. The doctor rose from his chair and walked around my bed as a nurse entered the hospital room to take me back to the infant ward.

"Mr. and Mrs. Mengel, you must understand. We don't know if this will work or not. Andrew's body cannot tolerate meat, poultry, dairy, seafood or nuts. He does not have the enzyme in his liver to break it down. If he eats a normal diet, it will quickly become toxic to him and there will be disastrous effects."

"What happens then? What can we do to help him?" my father asked, pressing the medical staff for answers about his son.

My mother looked over at my father. "Andrew needs breast milk," she said, as he nodded. They both knew.

"How can Andrew get the protein his body needs?" my father asked. "Can he be breast fed?"

"We cannot recommend that," the doctor said. "And we also cannot recommend this treatment."

My father stood up. "Wait a minute. You are telling us that you don't recommend what you are recommending?"

The doctor shifted his feet and stammered. "You see, Mr. Mengel…"

My father shook his head. "No, doctor. *This is our child.* You are telling us that he has an abnormality in his liver and now needs all these special formulas and dietary restrictions. How long is this for?"

The doctor shrugged his shoulders, as he closed his binder, shoving a pen into his breast pocket.

"It's experimental," he said. "This diet we can place him on. And that is why if you choose to breast feed, I cannot recommend that to you. Andrew needs to be on this diet and follow it to the letter. This diet we have formulated is too new for any deviations. We just don't know what will happen. We don't know what the outcome may be, but there are studies currently underway, and we are hoping that this protein restricted diet will allow his brain to develop normally."

"But you cannot recommend breast feeding to us? Why not?" my father asked. "Doesn't the brain need the cerebrosides?"

The doctor moved closer to the bed, and my parents raised their eyes, staring at him and watching his every move. He sat his clipboard down at the foot of the bed, near my mother's feet, concealed by the heavy blanket. He pursed his lips, holding his chin.

"We know nothing," he finally said.

His movements were careful and slow.

"Well, correct that. We know little. Some. But if Andrew consumes the protein that is in most foods, his liver will not be able to process it, Mr. and Mrs. Mengel. The phenylalanine will build up to toxic levels in his bloodstream, and he will experience the effects of high blood phe levels."

92

"Blood *phe*?" my mother asked, looking up.

The doctor extended his arms and pressed his palms outwards as he nodded. "Yes, yes. Pronounced like a fee for a credit card. At least that's how we abbreviate it. But with PKU, the spelling of the word is different, and it holds a very different meaning. But I was getting to that. We use the term 'phe' as an abbreviation for phenylalanine. That is what Andrew is allergic to, because his liver is missing the enzyme needed to break down the protein into what his body can use, and the phe builds up in his blood. If that happens, he will experience the symptoms of untreated PKU."

My father took a breath and sighed, looking over at my mother. He stood and looked directly at the doctor. "And what are those?"

"He will be mentally impaired, Mr. Mengel. Assistance for life. Skin conditions, neurological problems. Possibly seizures. Poor judgement, more."

My mother raised her head and looked up at the doctor. "Bring us our son back."

The doctor turned, gestured to the nurse, and she scurried out of the room. "Mr. and Mrs. Mengel," he said. "Babies can develop a musty odor when their blood levels are elevated, and tend to be colicky and cry, almost inconsolably."

My parents looked at each other with knowing glances.

My mother raised her arms as the nurse returned with me. "It's no wonder," my mom said, wrapping me up in a blanket and holding me close to her chest. "Andrew has been crying a lot lately, hon." My father nodded, and she was right. During my first two weeks of life, I was breast fed, and I was crying almost constantly.

"There was nothing we've been able to do to calm Andrew," my father said, looking at the medical staff which began gathering around the bedside. "We've tried everything."

The doctor nodded.

"Yes," he said. "Andrew's blood phe levels, when we tested them, are 47. Because you have been raising him on breast milk. To put things into perspective, safe blood phe levels are 2 to 4. This is certain to cause him severe brain damage. *You must stop breast feeding him immediately.*"

My parents looked at each other, and then down at me. I was finally sleeping in my mother's arms. My cheeks were still red from my recent crying; I had my thumb in my mouth, and for the time being, I was seemingly content.

Could I have been mentally challenged?

Overly careful and circumspect?

Would there be a period when my care would reach beyond the ability of my parents and siblings?

What would happen if they weren't there?

There were so many questions during that time, and I didn't start asking them myself until I became an adult.

When I was still a child, perhaps ten, maybe twelve, I carried my big silver boom box while wearing a grey sweat suit through the thick trees in front of my house to the street where the neighborhood children were playing. It had big, round, black speakers and the boom boxes were all the rage in those days for kids my age.

I brought the dull, silver box playing *Thriller*, mostly, as it was my favorite. I dragged the box with me, carrying it as I watched the other kids' movement through the trees.

This will make me cool, I thought. *This will make me like them.*

I don't know how my mother afforded the silver boom box, but I do remember how elated I was to have opened it on Christmas morning. I had all of the cassettes, as I waited for the Michael Jackson songs to play on the radio, as I recorded them and made my own tapes of his hits. I loved playing them on my new boom box. I looked down at the big portable stereo with the long, slender handle, and then at the small cassette in my hand.

It was a new mixtape I made, recording the songs from the radio, making every effort to cut out the DJ's chatter. I remember the frustration when the DJ talks during the opening of the songs. I wanted it to be just like a real tape if I'd bought a Michael Jackson cassette in the store. But I couldn't afford that, so I made my own. But standing in the trees with the stereo I held, I had a complete tape of the music I loved, with the small, carboard insert in the hard plastic case. I wrote with the best penmanship I could to inform of songs on the tape, as I looked at it while I stood in the woods, watching the neighborhood boys playing in the street.

Jeff and Kevin were there, close to my age, although neither of them went to the same middle school as me. I went to the Catholic school with the nuns, and they went to the public schools. I wore a uniform; they got to wear whatever they wanted.

I remember wishing I could too.

This is my chance, I thought.

Kevin was always a good friend, but now Jeff was there as well.

I could feel the knot build in my stomach as I watched Jeff grab the basketball from Kevin, running and jumping, sinking it into the basket.

Kevin laughed and congratulated him, but Jeff was the athlete, gruff and commanding. His mother was also a single parent, raising him, and his brother, but Jeff usually was a neighbor I would choose to avoid.

I looked down, as the silver shell of my radio gleamed in the fading sunlight. *But I have this now,* I thought. *Now he will be nice to me.* Kevin was always nice to me, a true friend. Jeff, on the other hand, was aggressive and unpredictable.

Dried, brown leaves crunched under my sneakers as I took slow, careful steps and emerged from the woods, until I saw Jeff's face.

His eyes were wide and stern.

"What are *you* doing here, Andrew?"

I stopped in my tracks. Michael Jackson's "Beat It" was playing on the boom box, and I shifted it from one hand to the other. "I wanted to show you my new boom box," I said. "My mom got it for me last Christmas."

Jeff scoffed and tossed the basketball down. It bounced away as he approached me. He pushed me on the chest. "Why are you here?"

"I – "

I looked over at Kevin. "Jeff, come on," he said. "Don't push him. He's just wants to be our friend."

Jeff turned and bent down to grab the basketball. "He's a fuckin' *weirdo.*" He bounced the basketball as Kevin retrieved it. He watched Jeff, shaking his head, as he started dribbling.

"Come on, man," Kevin said. "Lighten up on him. He's just trying to play with us."

Jeff looked down at the boom box and scoffed. "So, your mom got that for you?"

I nodded.

"You couldn't even get the real tape?"

I looked down at my mix tape. Maybe Jeff was right. It was just a simple K-Mart cassette I got for ninety-nine cents and recorded the songs off the radio.

"My mom made me spend the night over there," Jeff said, with a sense of disgust as he grabbed the ball from Kevin. "They didn't even have the air conditioning on. We had a bunch of fans."

I slowly turned to go back through the woods, back to my house. Maybe this wasn't such a good idea. I sighed as I shifted my boom box from one arm to the other.

"Yeah go," he said. "You're a frickin' *retard*. We don't want to hang out with *you*, you *dumbbell*."

There was something about those words.

Sometimes, the words come and are meaningless. And from others, when they are spoken, they sting like the pierce of criticism and contempt.

And rejection.

When that assault is thrust upon someone, it might be prudent to stonewall them. For that day, and with that boom box, I continued that desire to be accepted. By those who were in my life for some reason or purpose, which I had yet to understand. Now, decades later, as I write and remember this, I know that there were those who were inserted in my life, not to support me in the same way my angels did, my family.

The others were there to make me stronger.

To embrace my difference.

But, as a ten-year-old boy, I was heartbroken. I just wanted some friends. And I was saddened that I couldn't have them, but the rejection stung like a wasp.

So, I left.

I didn't think much about it then. I never really considered Jeff a friend per se, but, of course, with my type of personality, I would reach out to anyone to form a friendship. I know there was a lot of anger in his household.

His older brother bullied him, at least that's what I had heard and remembered. They moved away after a while. I never remembered why he spent the night over at our house that one night, and I will likely never know. I do know that my mother has always reached out to others in need, so I imagine there was some need that I could only speculate about.

Kevin, on the other hand, was more of a friend, and we grew up together on that street.

I remember the disappointment when I wasn't about to join their afternoon fun, but looking back on it, I understand why.

Kevin did what he could. Jeff was a bully, because he was bullied. Since then, in my adult life, I have recognized the importance of intolerance to bullying anyone, anywhere. It's wrong, and unacceptable. The bullies are hurting as well, but I try to spread awareness on my social media to celebrate all our differences. I can't help the bullies; they need to find the help that they require.

But I can celebrate.

Because we all need to be loved, we all need to feel special, and we all need to feel wanted and included. Like the needs we are born with, love and acceptance are paramount. And so that is one of the things I have chosen to celebrate as an author. Our differences.

Fitting in was tough, as it was for all of us.

And I did try to fit in, throughout my childhood. In retrospect, in my desperate attempts to fit in while attending school, I hadn't realized the tiny moments in my life which were destined to prepare me for something bigger and more life changing. It wasn't until I shared my true self with the world, and came out of the PKU closet, that I would be yearning for the difference from the norm. Everybody was doing this; everybody was doing that. If everyone went backward, I wanted to go forward. And if everyone went right, I would choose to go left.

My dancing shoes were always of a different style.

In the years when I was a young adult, it was far less common than it was when approaching middle age. During the time when the world's attention span seemed to lessen, and when the creativity accepted seemed to be increasingly visual, there have always been trends.

"I don't want to use trending music," I said, furiously typing a comment on the video I was watching with literary peers discussing marketing ideas. "I use what music speaks to me and works well with my brand. What works artistically. I don't like to jump on trends, although sometimes, we are forced to if we want to make a connection."

But in the years when I was a small boy, I didn't know that I really *craved* difference from the usual.

It was those small moments which became profound that spoke to me as I became an adult, sitting on the back screened porch on a warm winter afternoon in Florida, staring at my first manuscript length work. I read through it and studied it and rewrote it again and again for the better part of the year. My friends told me that I had to share it, but the trepidation set in.

Would the world appreciate the thoughts in my mind?

What would they say? Would anyone even care?

Or maybe sharing my deepest and most personal fears wasn't such a great idea, after all. I had dreamed, for years, of becoming an author.

Now, this was my chance. I had been working on the manuscript for many years. My best friend encouraged me to finish it.

I paused and I looked at the bright blue button that read "publish" as my heart rate quickened.

This was it.

Perhaps I could take this step in my journey.

It was now or never. I wanted to be somebody and have the world love me and remember me and listen to me and dreamed of becoming a published author.

This was my chance to cross the threshold, and my hand remained frozen.

Would the world like me?

For how much I embrace being different now, I understand why I made every effort to prevent others from knowing the big, deep, dark secret of PKU when I was child. There was so little known about the condition when I was boy that it seemed that I became a science experiment. It seemed I was always at the doctor.

I had to listen to nutritionists who instructed me what I could eat, and how much, and when. I would feel my heart race as the phone rang after my bloodwork appointments, for I knew that I would get the results, and the lectures.

The simple act of going to school was an anxiety inducing experience, and I remember my palms being wet when lunch hour approached, especially in high school.

I knew then that I wanted to avoid any types of events that were centered around food and eating. It was simply too much, and I didn't want to be a burden; I didn't want to be in the spotlight. And I didn't want people to ask questions, or fuss about what Andrew could eat.

Or could not eat. Or to have to run around, figuring out what to do, because I was there.

Since then, my perspective has changed.

I have learned how much food brings people together, and I have embraced that. I remember telling my parents that, when selecting a major in Hospitality Management for college, initially, that I did not want to do anything which involved food.

But I had no choice.

With that type of degree, I quickly learned that it was impossible, but that helped form my mindset when I approached adulthood, as by taking those required food-based courses, it unlocked a talent I have surrounding food which I was completely unaware of. And it was in the following years when, as an adult, when I then embraced food-focused gatherings, and the importance of breaking bread together.

Slowly, over the years, throughout adulthood, I became more acceptable of my PKU. It became easier to order in restaurants, and even though people did not know or understand what PKU was, they always knew that I had "some special diet" and I couldn't eat animal products.

I found that simplifying it a bit helped make it easier for people to understand who were not used to so many specifics which surrounded a metabolic disorder.

Over time, the stigma of being different lessened, and as I discovered that talent I had with writing, I started to want to bring my difference to the world.

CHAPTER FIVE

My mother has always been one of my biggest cheerleaders.

As I write this, she is battling COVID-19, in the time when the world has endured so much heartache and loss, and somehow, we all gained hope for something better. Her presence during those times, although we were located in separate states on opposite ends of the country, was like the sliver of light that reaches downwards through a layer of darkened clouds.

Still, I felt helpless, to a degree, when I learned she had contracted the illness from which we were all sheltering from.

Yet, to have an illness, which invades the body like the stain of sin on humans, there was a certain purpose for which we were all meant. There certainly is a reason for all of us to be here, on this planet, soaring through the cosmos. A path lies before each of us, and our journey takes us to each step required for our purpose.

My mother has always been the caretaker, as she has followed her life's calling by working for decades in the assistance of developmentally disabled individuals.

She also cared for her entire family, and children and grandchildren, and, quite importantly, me.

Even in recent interactions, and with the success I have experienced, a genuine tone of concern emits from her when my mother learns of the challenges that I sometimes continue to face in relation to treating my Phenylketonuria. She has always appreciated my desire to live a normal life, and she has never stood in the way of my desire to experience life as, somehow, I was meant to; taking the journey I was called to do. Regardless, the obstacles for PKU treatment continue, even when I may be entering the second half of my life.

In the years when I was writing *War Angel*, I felt much discouragement, as I do occasionally while working on a large-scale creative project. The books that I write do not always come so easily to me.

There were many phone calls while I was driving to my bartending job, discussing the plight of the world.

"We all need a war angel in our lives right about now," my mom said. It was something she said that had defined my life moving ahead. And while my writing career would not take a step forward until years later, when looking back, I now understand what she was trying to tell me.

Also, when I was writing *War Angel*, the deadliest terror attack on American soil since 9/11, at the time, took place a mere few miles from my house at the Pulse Nightclub in Orlando, Florida. I was there to ring in the New Year with friends previously.

I still remember the three-a.m. phone call I received from my best friend like it was yesterday. He was out of town at the time and was calling to check on my well-being. As time progressed, the conversation in the call rang through my thoughts for years after.

"Are you okay?"

I tried to brush the sleep off.

I had fallen asleep on the couch and the dogs lounged at my feet. "Yeah, of course I'm okay. Why wouldn't I be?"

"There's just been a massacre at Pulse."

I swung my legs to the floor as I rubbed sleep from my eyes. "What?! You're kidding me." I reached for the remote, snapped the TV on, and watched as dozens of emergency vehicles were littered around the area where the nightclub was, as their bright red and blue lights flashed against the dark night.

My mouth dropped open and I shook my head, as I listened to my friend fill me in on the news, all of which took place in the hours I was sleeping peacefully on the couch.

I couldn't believe it.

A mere few miles down the road, and at a business I had patronized recently.

"Were you sleeping?"

I nodded, although there was no way he could see me. "Yeah, I was. Crashed on the couch." I stared at the television in disbelief, shaking my head, and listening to my closest friend express his own disbelief.

I could have been there.

But I wasn't.

The horrors of that night frequently carry me back to my childhood. Those who died at Pulse also had their childhoods, and their memories, and their own journeys, which were cut short, brutally, by an AR-15.

I still frequently think back and cherish those first nights when I was a small boy, just discovering the world, and all it had to offer. It saddens me that others would not be able to afford that opportunity to remember their past, but I remain grateful for my own gifts and saddened for their loss.

I consider myself quite fortunate to place my puzzle pieces together. Not everyone is afforded that opportunity.

And I remembered. The thoughts always entered my mind.

It was then, in the distant past, on that frigid New Year's night, when I was still a young boy, when we sat ringing in 1982, and I was excited to watch the ball drop.

The windows were dark, yet the snow reflected the blue moonlight as I cupped my hands around my face and looked out the window.

I turned as we gathered around the television with my mother and siblings, watching the newscasters and revelers huddled in coats and scarves in Times Square. Tiny clouds of white vapor emitted from their mouths in the frigid night air as they talked and rejoiced in another year, another chance to correct our past mistakes, with an opportunity to strive to do better in the future.

A friend of my mother's gathered with us around the television as a warm fire crackled in the fireplace.

He seemed like an old man to me; but he probably was middle aged. "Happy New Year, Hank," my mother said, as their glasses clinked together. Hank stood in the center of the room, a small, soft-spoken man. "Andrew, come let me give you a hug and wish you a Happy New Year."

He seemed tall to me, but he was smaller than my mother. He spoke with a sweet, reassuring tone to his voice. He bent down and gave me a hug, and then a quick peck on the cheek.

I squirmed from him. "Ewww! *Boys don't kiss boys!*"

"Sure, they do," Hank said. He gave me a smile and patted me on the head.

Hank was always a friend to the family, sweet and alone and older, and sometimes he would come over for dinner. His heart attack came later that year, and on the day he was in surgery, my mom drove me home from school, as we passed his small apartment in a wooded area of cabins, she explained what had happened to him to me.

"Hank used to eat fast food every day," she said, shaking her head, staring at the road. "He had to have a quintuple bypass."

I gasped as I sat next to her, looking up at her as she looked forward, focusing on the road. "What's *that*?"

"It's when they open your chest and stop your heart," she said. "They cut into your chest and use a contraption to open your chest and spread your ribs apart so they can reach your heart. They hook you up to a machine to pump blood through your body so you can still be alive. They do this when people have their arteries clogged and they need to be fixed."

I gasped. "They stop your *heart*?!"

She nodded and flicked the turn signal on.

There was something about the heart not beating that was profound, even to my young mind. Back in those days when I was still a small boy, my

113

heart seemed insignificant to me. I was completely unaware of its presence.

Yet as we all know, without it, we would not live.

I better understand it now, and the enormous gravity of one's heart not beating on its own. I now am familiar with the entire bypass procedure as I write this, as a middle-aged man, several years after my own father's bypass.

In more recent years, the heart has been on the mind once again.

I remember receiving the call about my father's heart attack procedure from my stepsister; initially, my stepmother called us, early in the morning, and it was touch and go for a few days, while we waited for the surgery. And then my stepsister provided the news on the day of the procedure.

"He's off of bypass," she said. I could hear the relief in her voice. "His heart is beating on its own again!"

I rose from my chair slowly, as I was sitting on the lanai at my house in Florida. The manuscript I was working on fell into the background of my mind, as I listened intently to my stepsister.

"They are taking him to the ICU, and he will be there for a while to make sure there are no post-surgical complications," she said.

I felt the emotion build within my chest and my eyes swelled with tears.

I expressed my relief as well and discussed what was expected in the coming days. It was during the COVID pandemic, and travel out of state to visit was impossible. I felt helpless over 1,000 miles away, but the least I could do was stay in touch.

But his heart was beating.

That is what was most important.

I felt as if someone had turned a valve to let the air out of my body and I could relax again. I felt the warmth, and the stream of a tear glide down my cheek.

That was all that mattered at that moment.

My father's heart was beating on its own again.

I couldn't believe how profound those four words were, but they hit me like a freight train.

He's off of bypass.

I collapsed in a nearby chair and felt the waves of emotion rush through my body, placing my hand on my chest.

My own heart was racing.

In the following days, my father was on the mend, and the local news was predicting a Saharan dust cloud to move across the Atlantic and settle over Florida, and as I was attempting to resume my normal activities of writing, I felt a headache coming on.

I brushed it off, believing that my allergies were getting the best of me due to the dryness and dust in the air. I continued my writing, although concentration was fleeting with the headache building.

When I woke on the third day, I started seeing what I can only describe as the auras of small, colorful and faint "pinwheels" in my field of sight, and I thought I might be having a migraine. I had never experienced the auras before in my life, and I immediately thought it was that horrendous headache, brought on from the Saharan dust that had invaded the area.

I never thought that it might be something else.

The next day, Sunday morning, after I had learned that my father was recovering from his Bypass surgery, I woke up, swung my legs to the floor, and my headache was still there. It was now on its fourth day. I had never experienced a headache that was days long in my entire life, and I was starting to think that maybe

I should schedule a doctor's appointment. I still had my health insurance from the bar I worked at that closed when the pandemic brought the entire world to its knees; I considered myself lucky at that point. Yet as I made my way downstairs, I started to feel lightheaded.

We snapped the tv on and I sat in the recliner, figuring I would take the dogs on a walk shortly, and as I started the normal morning chat with my best friend and housemate, the room started to spin. It felt as if I were drunk, yet it was early in the morning, and I didn't have anything to drink at all, let alone any alcohol.

But I chose not to say anything.

It would pass. The strange feeling would pass. *I'm just a little lightheaded*, I thought. *I probably need to eat something.*

And the feeling, what I learned was vertigo, passed after a few moments. I headed into the kitchen, grabbed the leashes, and hooked up the dogs for their walks. I grabbed my face mask and headed out into the Florida summer heat and humidity.

I said a prayer.

I started to feel like something was wrong. But I was hoping that these feelings would pass; that the headache would ease, and that I could move on with my life. I'd had periods of hypochondria in my younger years, which I have always suspected were somehow connected to my Phenylketonuria; however, this time it was different.

My symptoms were real.

While walking the dogs, I unhooked the mask off my ear and let it hang down from my other ear, as I caught my breath and let my face cool.

Had it always been this difficult to walk the dogs in the summer humidity? Was I always out of breath like this?

I felt like I had to catch my breath. But I pressed on. I seemed to be feeling okay. The dogs stayed with me, as if they knew something was a little off about their daddy, but finally we made it back to the house.

"I am going up to take a shower," I told my best friend, as the dogs padded their way through the house, seeking the water dish, their nails clicking on the hardwood. "I am drenched," I said, as I headed up the stairs.

The feeling of uncertainty washed through me as I took each step, and the anxiety grew as I turned the water on in the shower. I brought my fingers up to my temples, gently massaging them. Why won't this headache go away? I thought.

I tried to brush it off.

I stood under the hot water for a few moments, relishing the temporary relief of the head pain, bent down, and reached for the shampoo. I squeezed a glob in my palm, and tilted my head back…

We're back!

Did you miss us? We are the three letters that follow you everywhere. Care for a little reminder? Now you can't escape us. For the shit has gotten real. It is your destiny to carry us with you. We are your cross. We are the weight of your shadows. And we always know your thoughts.

I braced myself on the side of the shower.

As I looked up, everything seemed to bend, right in my field of vision. I turned my head to the right. There were too many bottles of shampoo. Everything was bending as I moved my head, moving, as if I had turned into a kaleidoscope.

I could feel my heart racing.

I knew I needed to be seen by a doctor. Now this was for real. I hastily washed the shampoo from my head, grasped the side wall of the shower, and reached down towards the handle. There were several, and they all seemed to be moving in front of me, dancing for me. I reached outwards, searching for the handle, finally grabbing it, turning it and stopping the water.

I eased myself out of the shower, holding myself as steady as I could. Somehow, I managed to grab a towel and make it down the hallway towards my room.

And then, just as quickly as it had started, my vision returned to normal.

I looked around, wondering what had just happened. My vision had never doubled like that before, and I knew, deep down, that something was wrong. More so than it ever had been before.

I dried myself off as quickly as I could, as I felt anxiety washing through me.

I hadn't been to the doctor for a while, and I didn't know what to expect.

Could I have ignored the episode and pretended nothing had happened? Sure, I could have. And there were other times, in my past, when I did have what I thought were strange symptoms, and then I felt better, and I continued with my life, and nothing happened. Except some relief from my anxiety.

In this case, however, I knew I had to face this demon.

We are the dark shadows that follow you...

As I headed down the stairs, I heard my housemate at the sink and dishes clanking.

"Hey, I think I need to go to the hospital," I called down in a shaky voice, before I had even realized I blurted my thoughts out.

I heard the faucet shut off.

"Okay," he said. "Come on girls, let's go to the room."

I quietly put my shoes on as he herded the dogs into the room that they were staying in when we left the house. He locked up, and we headed out to the car.

"What's wrong?" he asked when we were in the car. As we backed up and the garage door closed, I took a breath and closed my eyes.

"All of a sudden, when I was taking a shower, my vision got all jacked up. It was like I was looking through a kaleidoscope."

"Woah. Is it still like that?"

I waved my hand as he navigated the car out towards the main thoroughfare. "No, no. It only lasted about thirty seconds. But I figured I needed to see a doctor. Like now."

"You want to go to an urgent care?"

"Just take me to the emergency room. Earlier, when you and I were chatting and watching the news, the room started spinning. Like I was trashed. But I didn't have anything to drink. I didn't say anything, but something feels wrong."

And there I was.

It was the height of the COVID pandemic, we had masks strapped across our faces, and we checked into a very classy yet deserted hospital emergency room early on Sunday morning. At that point in my life, I had thought that I had beaten the demon of hypochondria.

For that festering monster, I have said over the years, can keep one from medical care. But that day, the monster emerged from beneath the bed.

Throughout my childhood, my parents were dedicated to my health. And also, to the development of my mind, facing odds that many would have found overwhelming.

And on that day, when I stood in the emergency room, handing my ID card over to the receptionist, who asked me about my medical history, while she was furiously typing on the computer, I could feel the demon of anxiety had its full grip on me, and was not going to let go.

"Your blood pressure is 172 over 135," the triage nurse said. "It was probably higher when you had the vertigo and vision problems."

The numbers seemed high to me, and I even told the medical staff that the highest reading in my life to that date was 158 over 110, and that was when I was in my early thirties. That had been years prior.

As the doctors evaluated me, they ordered a CAT-scan, and when they returned me to my room, they asked if I was allergic to any medications.

"I have PKU," I said.

"Is it being treated?"

I hemmed and hawed.

"I've been looking for a clinic here, but it hasn't been going so well. But I have all my formulas. Everything I need. I just need a doctor to help keep my blood pressure under control, but who can also manage my PKU. I follow the diet. Since I was a child, I've learned how to manage the diet."

"When was your last phenylalanine level tested?"

"It's been a while."

The doctors nodded. "Okay. We are going to get your CAT-scan results, to make sure there's nothing going on in your brain, and in the meantime, we are going to give you a medication that will relax you and lower your blood pressure."

My housemate, my closest friend, looked up from his smartphone. "There's going to be nothing normal, doctor."

Everyone laughed and the mood lightened.

I didn't know if there would be something in my CAT scan results that would show a new journey for me. I felt the grip of my anxiety wrap its strength around me, but the results were clear. As the doctors discussed my blood pressure with me, and about my PKU diet, they recommended a doctor in the area who accepted my insurance, which I still had at the time, even though I was on furlough from my bartending job due to the pandemic.

"Things could have been very well worse for you," the doctor said, closing my chart. They looked at the latest blood pressure reading. It was about 140. Not ideal, of course, but stable enough to discharge me. "You could have had a stroke, or worse."

And when I replay that morning in my mind, over and over, I do realize that I am meant to live. I have never had thoughts otherwise, but in this case, I fully understand that my housemate was there for a purpose.

And that morning, his purpose was to save me by acting fast.

Had he not been there, I know what would have happened. I would have chosen to lie down.

I would have become anxious about it, but I would have moved throughout the day as if it had not happened.

Yet it did.

And the events would remain in the back of my mind causing more anxiety, even if nothing further happened the rest of that life-changing day. But had my housemate not been there, had I chosen to ignore it and lie down, I was very well aware, and was told, that it could have been a precursor to a stroke. And in that case, I would have been alone. I would have been unable to save myself. I would have been unable to move.

And so yes, my life was saved that day, in every sense of the word.

CHAPTER SIX

The heart beats.

From the moment of birth until the moment of death, the heart is the center of our existence.

It beats, pumps blood throughout our body, and allows us to live, whether or not we are aware of its presence, or if we spend each day working to preserve it.

Blood beats life in our bodies, and it is a measure of our daily existence.

But what does truly measure us?

The beat of a human heart? Or is it time? Can we catch time and preserve it, somehow?

We try to. We write books; we take photographs; we film videos. But what happens in the end?

Time moves on.

With, or without us.

It continues, in its own infinite journey. We talk about growing old with one another, but what happens when things, but more so, people, start to drift away from us? We reach out to hold on to them, to keep those who we cherish, those living beings, close to us, for as long as we can.

But eventually, our grip loosens.

And we are unable to keep holding on and must face the journey from a new perspective. We must face the future without what, or who we had with us before.

The stepping stones remain in front of us, regardless of how far we may be on the path. When we turn, and look behind us, we see the past, and the consequences – or the benefits – of our choices.

As the shoreline becomes distant and increasingly difficult to see, we realize that there are those who remain in our past; they become the ghosts we cling to, for advice, leadership, and guidance, whether it be a lesson we learned by knowing them, or a serendipitous reason they were a part of our journey. As those memories help form our new direction, and choose our forward path, as it slowly reveals itself.

Still, the heart beats, and the blood remains within us, flowing through us, bringing us to our destinies.

But could the blood betray us? Perhaps it could. The anxiety of receiving poor test results, or a phobia of the pain of needles.

I was a child of no more than five.

My mother held me in her lap, as we leaned on the cool porcelain. Those days sitting together on the floor, leaning on the toilet, huddling in the bathroom, were frequent. They were dreaded, and they were necessary.

And they pierced me with pain.

I squirmed in her arms. "No, no, *no please!*"

Her face fell, knowing her child, her baby, was in sheer terror. "Andrew, we must test your blood. We have to see how we are doing."

It was the lancet.

Silver and reflecting the light, ready to pierce my finger, and send pain through a young boy's body which should not be experienced.

But that is all we had back then.

She held me tighter as I squirmed and fought.

"No, no! Not that *please!*" I pleaded with her. "*Please, please, please!* If we don't do it, I will eat everything right. I will do everything right." The warmth of tears streamed down my cheeks as I saw the lancet, my eyes wide with terror.

My mother held it between her forefinger and thumb, and it glistened in the light coming from above the nearby sink. The lancet looked like a small shiny pointed arrow, and the only way the test could happen is by a finger jab.

My mother hugged me as we leaned against the wall, and I could feel the warmth of tears on her cheek as I leaned against her. Who would want to hurt their child?

She didn't want to do this either, but it was necessary. The only way. I never wanted it to be done. But the blood had to be tested. We had to know how I was doing, how the levels were.

Because the mind had to be preserved.

I was subjected to a series of regular blood tests throughout childhood; I also am supposed to test my blood regularly as a PKU adult as well, but I seem to have developed a blood and needle phobia from those experiences.

Test anxiety from the fear of poor results, and that has filtered to my adult life as well, as getting myself to go to the doctor on a regular basis is something I must continue to cheer myself on for.

If I am not feeling well, I will go.

But I feel fine, going to the doctor was, especially in my young adult years, the furthest thing in my mind.

When I was receiving the follow-up bloodwork at a local lab after my emergency room visit, I was so anxious when they called my name in for the blood drawing that I was shaking.

I drank black coffee that morning, but nothing else. And the phlebotomist scolded me for doing that.

"It says on here no food or drink for this bloodwork."

I shrugged my shoulders. "I just had some black coffee."

She pursed her lips as she was snapping the gloves on her hands. "It didn't say coffee."

Her voice had an edge. "It only said water. I am going to make a note on your chart that you had cups of coffee this morning."

Well, she seemed pleasant.

As I sat in the chair, my sleeve rolled up and my left arm stretched outwards on the arm of the chair, I watched her gather the vials and place the apparatus on the table.

My palms were sweating again.

"This just makes me so nervous," I said.

She smiled and warmed up a bit. "It's just a little needle. Only a pinch at the most."

"But all those vials?"

"Well, I have to follow the bloodwork, and you are getting a complete CBC and a metabolic profile."

I tried to remember the paperwork I studied.

"Complete blood count," I said as she nodded. Great. Now we were checking under the hood when it had been eons since I'd been to the mechanic.

Any type of bad results – for anything – seemed incomprehensible. Did I fail the efforts of my family? The thoughts raced through my mind, and then I saw an image of my mother, holding me in the bathroom as a little boy, smoothing my hair and wiping the tears from my cheeks.

I might have failed *her*.

I leaned back in the chair, took a deep breath, and slowly exhaled, trying to brush the thoughts away, as the phlebotomist wiped some rubbing alcohol on my arm. "You know," I said. "I am sure you don't know this, but I am an author."

Her eyebrows rose and she cocked her head to the side, holding the needle, beaming. "Really! What have you written?"

I chuckled sheepishly. "Well, you may find this a bit funny. I wrote a supernatural thriller called *The Blood Decanter*."

She scoffed, shook her head and let out a chuckle. "So, you know there's nothing to this, right? Just a little prick, about a minute, and we're all done. But you wrote a book about blood?!"

I nodded. "I sure did."

As I focused on her and the conversation, she continued. "I do find it a little funny that you say you're so nervous, yet you wrote that book. But, who's to say, right?"

"Yeah, that's true. For sure." I leaned my head back, musing and smiling. "That almost sounds like a Tweet. *Author of The Blood Decanter terrified of bloodwork.*" I laughed, closing my eyes, and shaking my head back and forth a bit as she chuckled again.

I looked up and she nodded slowly, focused for a moment on what she was doing. "But you know what they say," she said.

"What's that?"

"People like you…authors. You guys who write scary books. You write about what scares *you*. That's what makes 'em good."

I nodded. "Yeah, that can be true. Okay, let's get this over with."

"Oh, you're fine!" she said, releasing the small rubber tube on my arm. "It's already done. Hey. And if it means anything to you, I'm the same way. I work with blood all day, but when it's my turn to get tested, I'm a nervous wreck!"

I let out a chuckle and got on with my day. Maybe that's all that was needed. That sense of normalcy. We must all go to the doctor and often require blood tests so the medical team can determine our needs.

Yet at that moment, at a time when I felt the terror piercing within me, I found the connection I needed to get past it. And when I emerged from the lab shortly after and headed to my car, I could feel the relief washing over me.

$$\mathcal{LL}$$

During the nostalgic decade of my childhood, when my favorite musical artists were Prince, Madonna, and Michael Jackson, I was in high school.

I used to write short stories on notebook paper and rip the "dog ears" (some call them "rabbit ears") off and drop them to the floor below my classroom desk. I didn't pay much attention to the missing enzyme in my liver because I didn't feel sick and I didn't feel anything.

My blood tests were taken regularly at the doctor's office with a needle to the arm, and we were long past the days of the horrid lancets and the hours leaning on the cool porcelain toilet in mom's lap.

There were aspects of my life that seemed perfectly normal to me.

Others, not so much.

When I explain it to someone outside of the family or the medical field, it often would be perceived as rather quite bizarre. "How can you not eat meat?" they would ask. "You *drink* your protein?! How is that *possible*?!" Those were the questions I would receive at just about every meal I had at school, or at a friend's house, or at a restaurant, or a gathering, a wedding, or a picnic.

The list goes on.

I became tired of explaining.

In the years before eating healthy, or vegan, or gluten free was trendy, I was fielding questions from friends, acquaintances and even strangers who would wonder why I was eating "special foods", why I would drink a weird, smelly thick drink to get my protein, and why I had to get my blood tested weekly to make sure I was managing my diet properly.

And I am different.

I always was.

In my own mind, I never realized I was different until others told me so. In the years since I learned about my Phenylketonuria, and its constant threat to my mind and central nervous system, I have learned much about myself.

But in those days, when I was a small boy, wondering about this funny sounding word which seemed to be such a large part of my life, I simply wanted to fit in.

And be loved.

And accepted.

And valued.

I wanted friends who *wanted* to spend time with me, for me; sharing a common bond with interests we would experience together and just be *normal*. I didn't want to be special when I was that age. I didn't want to be different. I didn't want to be unique, and I didn't want to have anyone else around like me. Yet, I was completely unaware that being different can be rather exceptional.

And extraordinary.

Regardless, during those years, I simply wanted to be like everyone else.

I didn't want the funny sounding condition called Phenylketonuria, which my parents and my siblings and my doctors all called "PKU" for short.

That was not for me.

It took me many years of self-discovery to better understand the asset which I had. My state of mind was constantly threatened by PKU, yet we managed.

We built my mind, brick by brick, with the masonry of my treatment – a diet which even the doctor's did not know would work. Even during the teenage years, when I was rebelling against the diet, in my period of wondering and doubt, somehow, my mind was still preserved.

I did not get the irreversible brain damage which the doctors sternly warned about.

My mother and father were stalwart in ensuring I received the cerebrosides from the breast milk – high in protein and potentially dangerous – yet my mind developed without much interference. Even when I was not listening to the doctors and nutritionists, overall, I would get right back on the path I was supposed to be on.

PKU.

Those letters were always in front of me, like giant stones, impeding my journey. Mountains which I must scale and climb to proceed.

Those three letters which had become a part of my life early in my life. Before I could recite the alphabet, I was already quite familiar with those three letters. It was those letters that not only made my life different, but as I looked backwards in time, and spoke with those in my life who are still living and examining everything about my life, I understood.

It was always these three letters, which dictate how I eat and live, which led me to see how being different can become quite extraordinary.

It was the PKU which seemed to define me in earlier years, and now, as an adult, I refuse to let their definitions of me continue as they did when I was a child.

I may be different, but I now know I am unique.

As we all are, we are exceptional.

There is no one else in the entire vastness of interstellar space that is quite like us, and despite our similarities, which will always occur, there will never be another person exactly the same as me, or you, or anyone else, in the entire history and future of the world.

ℒ

I've learned, but it has taken me decades, that I can be different; that it's okay.

In more recent years as an adult, I have craved being different, separating myself from others. Seeing that PKU is not always the heavy cross which I must carry throughout my entire life, as there is no cure for the condition.

Having PKU has taught me that it is a condition which carves my destiny for me. What I have always thought was a burden may actually be a definition of the formation of my character.

I was raised to care for myself and others.

But it does bring a sense that this was my destiny; I was meant to be different, I was meant to be special, and I was meant to carry the cross. Yet as I write this, as a middle-aged man, I have come to the realization that a burden can, at times, become a gift.

The daily challenges of caring for a special needs child, or perhaps for an aging parent, can allow us all to fully realize the cycle of life, and how time can be gained. To understand; to help someone on their own journey which they cannot take alone. Being there for them, as part of their journey, brings a sense of purpose.

And, as it may be, mostly to love them.

When my grandmother moved in with us, and she was diagnosed with Alzheimer's disease, I could see and remember the additional burden it placed on my mother, who was already raising me, my brother, and sister as a single parent, in addition to managing the unique challenge of my PKU, which is not curable.

During my high school years, I strayed from the doctrines, and it was the first time in my life when questions about my future entered.

Yet, as my grandmother declined, I saw the additional heaviness of the weight added to my mother's cross.

Still, while she was enduring nights when my grandmother would wander, or call the police, or think that we were all murdered somewhere, or slowly forget who we were – my mother, I suspect, would not trade that time with *her* mother for anything.

Would she have preferred that her mother not declined and slowly forgot who she was?

Certainly.

But that was a period in my mother's life when she was compelled and allowed to give her own mother the same loving care that she received as a child. Once an adult and twice a child, my best friend's grandmother Louise used to say, and the saying rings true, for all of us.

I make every attempt, in my own life, to process what we all must face as human beings. The loss that will, inevitably, one day come. I try to imagine life without my parents, or my siblings, or my closest friends, or my dogs.

And it remains difficult to imagine.

But like all of us, I will one day have to face life without them. Or they will have to face life without me.

I was given the burden of PKU, and, as a result, I have a special and close connection with my mother, as well as my father, and many people I know are not as close with their parents.

I consider myself lucky to be close with them.

I consider any closeness with another human being a gift. But I must remain with fortitude, as even though I am an adult, I have those thoughts dreading loss; and I fear the feelings, and the inevitable. Which we all must face.

But like all of us, I have lost before as well.

And it's at night when I feel most connected to those who have made it to the final step before me.

Not when I am dreaming as many do; although, sometimes, I dream of lost relatives and pets. In more recent years, I remember feeling a dog rubbing against my leg, when I was alone in the house. My housemate was traveling, and our new puppy was sleeping on the bed in the back room. I was walking through the front room talking on the phone with my mother.

I paused in the conversation.

It felt like a dog had rubbed up against my leg. Maybe our new puppy had emerged from her nap, and I had mentioned that to my mother. And then I looked down.

There was nothing there.

"This is weird, mom," I said. I hurried through the slender hallways beneath the soaring ceilings of the historic home that we were living in at the time and headed to the back room. Our new puppy was sleeping soundly on the bed.

I took a breath as I turned back towards the front of the house, which was shrouded in darkness, where I had been walking around, chatting with my mother who was now several states away, talking about the animals, when I distinctly felt a dog brush against my shin.

Perhaps a mid-sized dog. I thought it was our new puppy, who was also mid-sized. It was hard to tell. Yet our puppy was sleeping soundly on the bed at the opposite end of the house. I would have heard her nails clicking on the hardwood as she charged across the house. Certainly.

Yet I hadn't.

And still, I distinctly felt a dog rub up against me.

My mother and I started talking more about my first dog, a rescue, Inky, who died, suddenly and unexpectedly, at age nine.

She was a mixed breed, and my mother reminded me that she always waited for me on my bed, until she heard the school bus. And then Inky would come barreling downstairs, rushing to greet me with a wagging tail.

"Could it have been her?"

My mother hesitated for a moment. "I mean…it certainly could be. Your dog is still sleeping?"

"Yes," I said. "She has been the entire time I've been on the phone with you."

"Then I think you have your answer."

$\mathscr{LL}$

Throughout my fiction, I sometimes refer to an analogy which I have likened to life's journey.

This can apply to just about any type of journey, indeed – whether it be the quest for creating a family and building one's own personal legacy, or perhaps, a career, or creative venture, or even understanding a condition, which, when I was born, was little understood. Or anyone else's condition or cross they must carry as well. The diet I was placed on was supposed to protect my mind and nervous system, but it was a roll of the dice.

No one knew if it would really work.

A mere few years before I was born, there were others with my condition living in group homes with severe mental hindrance, requiring assistance throughout life. And my mother, father, and family were stalwart in protecting me from that; they carved a new destiny for me.

But as I write this, decades later, I have learned a lot about how normal I am.

Countless others have endured conditions – be medical or metabolic or otherwise – and, throughout their own lives, their journeys have, in many cases, been uncertain and fraught with turmoil with their own heavy crosses to carry. In that sense, I am probably somewhat normal.

I have learned about many of the other conditions which have afflicted others, including members of my own family; with conditions such as diabetes, Crohn's disease, gluten intolerance, among many others. PKU is extraordinarily rare; it's a recessive gene and a hereditary condition which is passed on by two "carriers". If a mother and a father, who both happen to be carriers of PKU, have a child, there is a 25% chance that the baby will test serum-positive for Phenylketonuria.

While there are genetic tests which can determine if you are a carrier, it is important to understand, in the early twenty-first century, that the uncertainty of learning that your newborn child has a potentially devastating metabolic condition is not the same as it was during the 1970's, when I arrived in the world. Currently, we know that the PKU diet works. But decades ago, there was much uncertainty which surrounded the condition.

We now are aware that the diet must be followed for life, as there remains no cure.

In the past, babies were taken off-diet after the early-childhood phase when the brain was then believed to have fully developed. However, over the course of the following decades, we have learned that the brain continues to develop well into the twenties. Additionally, for babies who are born the twenty-first century, the PKU condition is far better understood, with a variety of options of foods which someone with PKU *can* eat, such as low-protein meat alternatives and a various amount of supplementary formulas, which the patient will consume in conjunction with a low-protein diet, as the main affliction of PKU is a missing enzyme in the liver, which is responsible for the breakdown of protein into its absorbable essential amino acids.

But what exactly is Phenylketonuria?

And how does that make me different?

When I was a boy, it was those three letters which always followed me around.

PKU.

Those letters were the cross I was destined to carry; I was told the cross would be heavy. It was. And still is. The weight has never lightened; nor will it ever. I was different because of that cross, those three letters which quickly became part of my identity.

CHAPTER SEVEN

This book was written on the advice of several people in my life.

As I am considered a "poster child" for PKU, numerous people in my life encouraged me to write my story, to help others learn about this rare metabolic condition. This book is written not only to speak to those who also have the disorder, but also others who don't. Those who do not suffer from PKU, who can better understand why someone cannot have the food items they may have so lovingly prepared.

Most importantly, however, this book is for those younger than I am who may wonder if they, too, can lead a normal life.

There was no reason to hide my own true self.

I knew that PKU was what I had.

While we all have our ailments, our restrictions and limitations, I was not alone in experiencing a condition, even if it took me a while to realize it.

Yet when I would attend any type of event, dinner, luncheon, potluck or social centered around food, I would feel quite alone, for a good portion of my life. In the years that this book was written, it has become more commonplace – and even trendy – to limit one's diet and request special menu items in restaurants or at gatherings.

Yet, during the days when I was a boy, in the 1980's, and even in my young adulthood, it seemed far more unthinkable to request anything specially prepared in a restaurant.

But what about at a food-centered gathering?

I remember walking up to the table.

In Michigan in the early 1980's, PKU was a condition which was little understood in my own family, let alone among the general population. During that time, as a young boy, I remember attending a family wedding at my grandfather's house.

There was a large gathering at his home for the rehearsal dinner. There was a swimming pool, plenty of space for a group of many people, and plenty of room for the children to play, and the adults to socialize, and celebrate.

The dining room was set up for make-your-own deli sandwiches with a variety of breads and buns, with trays overflowing with mountains of chilled lunch meats, turkey, ham, salami, and a variety of cheeses and relish trays.

I stood at the table, holding a Styrofoam plate, biting my lower lip. I scanned the offerings nervously and looked up for anyone.

My father was busy with the other groomsmen at the rehearsal dinner for his brother's wedding, and I stood and watched as my other family members shuffled into the dining room.

They began piling meat, cheese, lettuce, and tomatoes on their sandwiches, slathering mayonnaise, and mustard on slices of variety of sliced breads.

Everyone was laughing, everyone was enjoying themselves, chatting boisterously, drinking cans of beer, and sipping on cocktails in plastic cups, and building their plates with piles of food. It was a day of fun and socializing.

It was a happy and joyous day because we were gathered for a wedding; my cousins dashed in between the adults, grabbing food from the table as their parents told them to get a plate.

I returned my attention to the table and the food.

There was a tray of pickles and olives. I slowly navigated the side of the table across from the others and looked at the bowl closest to me.

I loved potatoes, but my heart sank. I looked closely and saw the eggs and bacon. It was slathered in dairy.

Everything I was told that I couldn't have.

I slowly replaced the spoon.

The piles of lunch meats and cheeses were the most obvious forbidden foods on the table, but the potato salad was the most disappointing.

The laughter and chatter of the others faded away as they left the dining room to sit outside by the pool, and I remained there, alone, a small boy in the suddenly silent room, staring at the massive spread of food, with no one to guide me in my selections. The muffled voices coming from outside told me that I had to build my plate. Soon they would be wondering where I was.

Andrew would be missing.

I could hear the clock ticking in the nearby room and slowly reached for a pair of tongs. I put several black olives and a pickle spear on it, and for a moment, paused and stared at the bread selection. The olives rolled around as I scanned the table in desperation.

I could feel the anxiety build.

I knew I had to get back outside; it was time to sit and eat and play with my cousins. But I knew that time was passing. Despite being a small boy, I knew that the others were outside eating their sandwiches stuffed with meat, cheese, lettuce and tomatoes, and I wasn't supposed to eat regular bread.

I had to eat my special bread, which my parents made for me, as it had low protein content. But we didn't have it at this event.

I knew, even at the tender young age I was, that I could not eat two olives and a pickle. I selected a piece of rye bread, put in on a plate, and spread some bright yellow mustard on it, when my father appeared in the doorway behind me.

I turned around quickly.

"You can't have that bread Andrew," he said, approaching the table. "It has eggs in it." I looked up and watched him scanning it. "You can make yourself a salad," he said. I pointed to the potato salad and then the bowl of coleslaw. He leaned over the potato salad, taking the serving spoon, and examining it. His eyes fell as his face shifted, and he shook his head.

"There's bacon in this," he said. "And eggs." He looked over at me looking down and making direct eye contact. "You can't have the dairy anyway."

My father turned away from me as my uncle appeared in the doorway. "We need to find something that Andrew can eat," he said, shaking his head, with a sense of exasperation in his voice. "He can hardly have any of this."

My uncle nodded. "Oh sure!" he said cheerfully. "We have some fruit and Jell-O in the fridge. We can make him up a plate."

My uncle held out his hand and ushered me over to the kitchen. "Come on, sport. We'll find you something you can eat."

My father turned back to me. "You can get some of the lettuce and tomatoes over there, but you know you can't eat that bread. It has eggs and milk in it. Your uncle's going to get you some fruit. You can have some of the Jell-O, but only a little bit. That has protein in it."

I nodded slowly, taking my uncle's hand.

Back home, my mother would make me special Jell-O that she ordered from a place that my clinic and dietician had recommended. I enjoyed it, but it tasted different than regular Jell-O. Still, Jell-O was one of my favorite desserts.

I would always get excited when we took long road trips, and I got to select the large glass cup of Jell-O squares when we went to Ponderosa, my favorite restaurant as a boy. They offered an extensive salad bar with many selections, and I was able to make *choices*.

Yet at the rehearsal dinner with the deli sandwich displays, I struggled to find something to eat.

Everyone took so much time to figure out what I could eat for a simple meal, when I wanted to be out with my cousins, fitting in, and being normal with them. I didn't want all the fuss, yet, it had to be made. I had to eat *something.*

It wasn't when I was standing in the dining room, staring at a massive spread of food, panicking, trying to figure out how to put some food on my plate that I could have. It wasn't when my father came to my rescue to help me find something to eat, or when my uncle remembered the fruit which he had in the fridge. It was when I emerged from the house into the pool area, set up with round tables and tablecloths, filled with my extended family.

I held my plate of colorful fruit and Jell-O bright green salad and looked through the faded, white lace curtains which concealed the image of my extended family sitting at temporary tables scattered around the swimming pool on that summer evening. But I could see them. Their silhouettes, chatting and laughing; my older relatives would tilt their heads back in laughter, as when I scanned to the other side, where my cousins were sitting, I could see the outlines of their frames sitting around the table, as heads moved back and forth in a conversation which I was not privy to.

My father appeared and yanked the lacey curtain back.

Tables filled with my family members were scattered about the area. They were crowded and celebrating; laughing with each other, bonding with food. I saw the brilliant blue pool as a backdrop, and further down the side, the table with my cousins.

I slowly walked over to where all of them were sitting.

The other children looked up and saw me approaching with my paper plate of colorful fruit and salad. Their eyes widened and called across the pool, to their parents, who were eating, drinking and talking.

"Why don't we get *that*?!"

They pointed at my plate of bright and colorful fruits; watermelon, cantaloupe, grapes, and apples which were not placed on the dining room table with the other mountains of food. And the Jell-O. They pointed their fingers at me and called over to their parents.

I took a seat next to them; slowly, sheepishly, feeling my face grow hot. I didn't know how to answer. Why *did* I get these foods when they ate the same foods that their parents were having?

It was not something that I wanted to happen.

Other children my age didn't want their sandwiches and potato salad; they wanted what I had. "Andrew has to eat special food," some of my older cousins said. "He can't eat what you have." I took my small, plastic fork and poked at a bright red watermelon square as the other children turned their attention to me.

"Why do you have to eat special food?"

"What is wrong with you?"

"Why can't you eat what we're having?"

Why do you even care?

They fired the questions at me, having a natural reaction, overcome with childhood curiosity while experiencing someone who was different. They were inquisitive, they were excited.

And they were my own cousins.

At that point in my life, although I was younger than ten years old, I already held an understanding of what would have happened to me if I had chosen to ignore what my parents and doctors had told me. If I had helped myself to a sandwich piled with meats and cheeses like my cousins were able to. If I snuck off to an empty room with one of the deviled eggs from the platter.

Only if.

What would happen?

What would my mind do if I chose to ignore the directives? What would happen if I chose to eat the seemingly healthy food that everyone else was eating – except me?

Did the doctors know what they were talking about?

"In the beginning, we were just figuring it all out," my father said, decades later, while on a phone call discussing the memories which this book explores. "You must understand, Andrew, this was all very new. Before you were born, PKU didn't *have* a diet. They didn't *have* a test. They had no way to monitor it. You are truly a poster child for PKU. You are a success story. That's why you must write this book. With the people that have PKU now, no one else has that story. Your story. Which is unique in how your mind was created, and what you did with it. The entire medical community will probably make it required reading for their programs."

I considered his words and thought back to the day around the pool when my cousins were examining the contents on my plate. I could see the look in their eyes, wide and curious, longing for the colorful fruit that I was eating. Maybe some kids would have felt triumphant, eating something special that their cousins and siblings were not allowed to have. But for me, I would have rather had what they were having, so no one would fuss over me.

I was the special one.

I was a different one.

And although I ate my food, I finished my plate, my face remained hot and red as I could feel their eyes staring at me; I tried to pretend I didn't notice. I pretended that I didn't hear them talking about how they didn't want *their* food, they wanted *mine*. I didn't know then that one day I would be an author, and a king of playing pretend and telling stories.

But then, and at that time, it was all reality, and my wishing they could eat the same thing as I was. I didn't know how special I was. I didn't want to be special. I just wanted meal time to be over, so we could get back to other activities; I wanted to blend in once again, so I could stop being different.

Oh, how blissfully unaware I was in life back then.

But we follow you…we are your shadows…

Little did I know that I would soon discover how beautiful and life-changing being different truly was.

PART TWO

YOU ARE UNIQUE

CHAPTER EIGHT

Now, as I write this story, I sit back and try to remember.

I try to remember the days from my childhood. When everything was so much simpler. When life didn't seem to have worry, or stress, or heart attacks, or funerals, or fights, or violence.

When I used to play in the backyard, digging cities in the sand, with my plastic dump trucks and shovels, digging up wild blueberry bushes for my "trees" and lining my sand streets with them.

I try to remember the days when I had my first pet; a hamster named Macaroni, who found his way into the heating ducts one warm, summer afternoon. Over the years, I had many carnival goldfish that always seemed to die on me. I became quite proficient at toilet flushing funerals. And I had gerbils three different times; I always got them in pairs, and their names were Coke and Pepsi, Salt and Pepper, and War and Peace.

But with my first pet, Macaroni, we had an interesting ordeal when he escaped his cage.

The house I grew up in had those long, rectangular aluminum heating ducts that lined the ceiling in the basement.

When it was quiet, you could hear Macaroni scurrying back and forth; his tiny nails clicking against the metal above. It was my mother who had to call our neighbor to the rescue, for she was a single mother, and the neighbor, who was a very helpful man, and was very kind, came to our house; he was destined to become a Baptist minister.

We were worried he might find his way to the furnace.

And we finally did get Macaroni out of the heating ducts. He was reunited with his cage, his hamster wheel, his pellets, and his cardboard toilet paper tubes.

But as hamsters do, he died one day.

And I remember burying him in a small shoe box, not far from where I built my city in the sand. Under the oak trees, beneath the shaded canopy, I dug a small, square grave, as sunlight filtered down from above. I placed him in the ground in his shoe box, lined with a blanket of brown, crumbled leaves, which, to me, was a perfectly fitting hamster funeral.

It's those times that I try to remember.

For one day, I woke up.

And I was no longer that child.

I was middle aged, and I longed for those simple days again. I worry about things now. My anxiety.

My blood pressure. Finances. The daily grind.

My parents are getting older, and I am becoming worried about their care, when they continue to worry about mine.

But despite all that worry, there has always been a big thing in my life, something that has contributed to both the positives and the negatives.

And that is the metabolic disease that I was born with.

Phenylketonuria.

PKU.

Those letters sometimes will fade into the background because everything is what it is and is how it always was. Yet there remains no cure, no matter which year I may be in, so it remains in my life.

And the letters always follow me around, and despite what I may be doing at any point in my life, it reminds me that they are there.

Those three letters are always present, no matter what I may do to try to outrun them.

L

I don't remember much from my early childhood, when I was a child of less than five years old.

I think my first memory was receiving a red Matchbox firetruck for my fifth birthday in Michigan, just before we hit the road to New Jersey. In fact, I think the house was already packed and full of boxes. I have a vague memory of my aunts and uncles sitting around the dining room table, but one thing that I do remember about that birthday quite clearly – that red firetruck.

And I was so happy with it.

I was so happy with that house in Michigan, a split level.

With my friends and family there.

With the best friend I had made, another boy of five, who was destined to one day visit me on the east coast. But during that period, it was time for our family to leave, and to explore a new area, with new people, and new friends, and a different destiny.

And then we headed east, to New Jersey.

I still remember the new house, standing in the kitchen, before it was even fully finished.

The new carpet smell.

I remember the yard being dirt and mud when we moved in, because the sod had not been planted yet. I remember the pale green wooden trim around the windows and the white aluminum siding. I had no idea a house would figure into my journey so greatly. My little mind, in its genesis of development, did not know.

And in that house, where I was, several years later, sitting at the counter in the kitchen, on the other side of the counter, across from my mother, who was cleaning the dishes from dinner that evening.

I was still a small boy then.

I stared intensely staring at three glasses of cream-colored liquid. The glasses were small – these days, the glasses probably weren't much larger than shot glasses at a bar. But for a seven-year-old, they seemed huge.

And each of them was filled, to the brim, with the disgusting "milk" – also known as my PKU "formula", which I drank daily for the needed protein, yet without the elements I am severely allergic to and unable to digest.

"Drink your milk," my mother said, as she continued to clean the counters and finish the dishes from dinner. "You can't move from that stool until your milk is gone."

"But there are *three* glasses!"

She stopped what she was doing and looked down at me. "You chose to drink them all at once. You know you are supposed to have them throughout the day. Now drink your milk." I scoffed and lowered my chin on my arms looking at the small glasses.

I closely examined one of the glasses. My eyes grew wide with horror, and I looked up at her. I held my nose.

"What is *wrong*?" she asked.

"There's a lump! *There's a lump*!" I pointed at the glass, tears rimming my eyes. "I will throw up!"

My mother put down her towel and stopped washing the dishes. "Calm down. I will strain it."

And strain it, she did.

For that lump would have made me throw up.

Perhaps not literally, but when some of the powder did not fully mix with the water, the lumps would form, and I used to guzzle the formula, for the taste was sickeningly sweet and medicinal. There was something about the lumps that were in that formula that I detested; I used to have to drink the concoction every day, to replace the protein that I couldn't get from normal sources.

And it was my mother who ensured that I drank my formula, "my milk", each day, so I would develop into a normal and healthy child, and eventually, a healthy adult.

Those were the years when I protested considerably against what I would day learn was life.

169

It was then that I would develop into a normal and healthy adult as I did, and I have achieved, and am still achieving things in life, but the road has been rough.

Still, for every pothole I encountered, there also was some smooth pavement. Despite reservations that crept through my mind, I still, for the most part, listened to the doctors. Throughout my childhood, I continued to make my attempts to be as undetected as possible. My diet and special eating habits were always there, yet others who knew me still thought of me as different.

When I was growing up, people used to stay "There's just something about Andrew."

In those days, it was difficult to determine exactly what it was, but I remained different. It may have started earlier, but one of the earliest memories of my going my own way was in middle school. I was raised Catholic, and our mother wanted us to go to a private Catholic school, which had a tuition, but she felt that we would receive a better education than at a public school.

While that can be arguable, we did have nuns in the administration, and one of them, a much older lady, was in charge of the music and the choir, which I was a part of.

When we were to perform, that afternoon, we helped the janitors set up the small, steel-folding chairs in the gymnasium, which had served as the concert hall as well as the cafeteria. All the parents would be coming to watch our chorale concert, and Sister C. was at her tall, wooden piano, organizing her music pages.

She clapped her hands and turned to face us. "Alrighty, boys and girls! Get in place on the risers. We need to run through our numbers before your parents arrive!"

We stopped helping with the chairs and scurried to the front by the stage as Sister C. went to the piano.

We filed on the risers just in front of the stage, as Sister C. raised her finger, and turned to face us from her small piano bench in front of the first row of folding chairs. As she started playing her simple notes, all the children started singing the song together, including me.

We ran through seasonal holiday songs that we would be singing for the parents and families, as people started filing in the bay of wooden doors on the other side of the auditorium. As the small folding chairs slowly filled with families, we filed back into the small music room through a door on the front side of the gymnasium, up several steps to a small trailer which was the music room.

I waited, knowing my mother, brother, sister, and some family friends would be in the audience coming to watch me sing with the group of students.

We all sat in the trailer on the group of small, colorful plastic chairs which littered the center of the music room, surrounded by drums, cymbals, another piano and other musical instruments.

Sister C. stood in front of the trailer, in front of a long, black chalkboard. She clapped her hands. "Okay, children! You sang so well earlier. Now it's time to sing even better!"

There was a soft knock on the door. Sister C. turned as the door slowly opened. A small, elderly nun appeared in full habit. "They are ready to start," she said.

Sister C.'s face beamed as she faced all the students. "It's showtime, everyone!"

As we filed into the gymnasium, the parents and families cheered and clapped, and Sister C. walked to the center of the aisle, introducing our chorale show. One of the assistants sat at the piano and started playing as the applause swelled. I looked to my left and saw my mom, brother and sister, and some of my family friends.

This was my first performance.

As we took our places in front, standing on the small aluminum risers, I looked out at the crowd, as they patiently waited in row after row of metal folding chairs. When the music started, we started singing the holiday carols as a group, harmonizing in unison, as Sister C played the piano. Her head bobbed back and forth with the melody, and families in the audience stood and clapped and took Polaroids.

I started to get bored as the somber holiday songs continued, but eventually, they started to get more upbeat.

And I couldn't help myself.

I started dancing and swaying to the music, back and forth, spinning around as the audience cheered and laughed. I was so enthralled with my own feeling for the music that I never noticed Sister C. glancing over and giving me dirty looks, as she waved her hands in a feeble attempt to get me to stop, and fall in line with the other children.

When the number was completed, we all received a standing ovation.

Regardless of whether Sister C. enjoyed my performance or not, the audience absolutely loved it, and some of the students who were near me started dancing as well. My family told me, after the performance, that people were noticing Sister C.'s reaction.

But the crowd was going wild and loving every minute of the little boy who simply couldn't help but dance and sing to the music, for I knew that I could not listen to upbeat music without dancing.

LF

Decades later, I sat in my writing studio.

In more recent days, I wasn't thinking about the time at the wedding rehearsal dinner when I couldn't have anything on the table. I thought, when I sat down to start this book, that I had mastered the diet. It was a daily record, which at that point, I would keep in my mind, of what I ate, to determine how much more I could eat during the day, while keeping my blood levels within the safe range.

As an adult, I came to have a liking for beer.

I wanted to fit in with my family, which has a German and Polish heritage, and truly be the Mengel I felt I was destined to be. There was something about it which I couldn't quite explain, but I have always been proud of my heritage and my family, on both sides of the coin.

In the Mengel family, family gatherings and barbeques were always adorned with food, but most of it were food items that I could not have.

Regardless, I have always loved being a Mengel, and, as an adult, it became much easier to find something to eat.

And on the other side of the family, it is a family of artists and those who appreciate them.

Still, food always was something that brought the families together, and, while both sides became more aware of my dietary needs at times, when eating or drinking, I was always counting in my mind.

Back in the days by the pool, I had never dreamed that I would become an author.

Or become creative, or anything for that matter. In my childhood days, I had to overcome my uncertainty as a person and my anxiety with acceptance, and there was much more I needed to experience in the journey, which has been like others who are becoming adults and contributing to the world and the betterment of humankind.

Yet there was the exception to the journey.

The three letters that always followed me, no matter where life and people took me. As a child, I had no idea that I would one day be on a quest to be different.

I did not know who I was in those days. And even so, I am still learning.

I still am on a journey to discover who I have always been my entire life; whether it be how I would eat, what I would wear, what I would do.

How I would be remembered by others after I was gone.

Or who would join me on my life's journey.

I had so much to learn back in my childhood days, and, sometimes, still do.

I don't know if I really saw it then.

Like many youths, I had a confident feeling at times that may have been unfounded. Now that I look back, I might be considered naïve. Now, as an adult, I know that I had so much to learn along the way. As I write this, as a middle-aged man, I am approaching fifty.

In that time, I didn't overcome PKU.

No one ever truly can; it's a lifetime predicament. But I did learn to live with it, although those three letters have not been kind to me over the years. So many challenges; setbacks.

Yet still, there has been much to celebrate.

This book is a story. It's a success story.

I was one of the first babies tested for the metabolic disorder *Phenylketonuria*, known by the three-letter acronym "PKU".

We were all tested for the condition at birth, yet I was one of the few who came up positive.

It's not as common as diabetes, the condition only affects about one in 20,000 individuals, sometimes less, but still aggressive in nature in terms of its effects. When I was born, I was one of the first PKU babies to be placed on a strict low-protein diet, which, at the time, was thought to be the best solution to minimize the devasting effects on the brain and central nervous system which phenylalanine had on my body. What could I have done?

Babies born as little as ten years before me were not as lucky as I was.

In the 1960's and earlier, there was no diet which would manage the intake of phenylalanine, and, as a result, those babies had horrendous effects on their mental state and brain development. Many of them, if not all, suffered severe brain development issues, and many were classified as "severely mentally challenged." When phenylalanine builds up in the blood, it becomes toxic to the body. In severe cases, seizures can occur.

But I was lucky to have been born when I was.

When the diet was there, when we knew that restricting protein might possibly help the brain develop normally, at least in the early years of life, when the brain was developing and growing at a rapid pace, I was a newborn. My mother and father were the ones who were faced with the seemingly insurmountable questions, with the questions which the doctors could only speculate about. It was the life-encompassing mystery surrounding my future, and if my mind would survive the wrath of PKU.

My three letters have always been PKU.

My mind survived; I did not wind up in an assisted living group home, or a psychiatric hospital, or a prison, or a morgue. There were many things that could have overtaken my life had I not had the people in my life who ensured my path was the right one.

So, I did not do any of the negative things. I became an author.

ℒ

If it weren't for those three letters, I believe that I would never be where I am today.

If it wasn't for PKU, I would have never had a proactive family – who remains so to this day – who all understood, and continue to understand, the ramifications of PKU diet mismanagement, and the necessity of protecting the mind.

I didn't want to spend my life in an assisted living group home, which was a real and constant threat throughout my life, my childhood especially. But my family all took their parts in ensuring that my mind would develop normally, even if I protested. Even if I saw everyone else eating food that I could not have.

And possibly I will never be able to have, barring a scientific breakthrough, and the development of the enzyme that my liver has been missing since birth.

Could I simply receive a liver transplant?

I've asked myself that question before. I haven't asked the doctors. "Would a new liver enable me to eat a normal diet?"

In my mind's eye, I saw myself asking that question. Yet when at the appointments, I never spoke up. Why, you ask me?

Because that wouldn't solve the problem.

Technically, there have been case studies where a transplanted liver has, essentially, cured PKU in a patient who received a new liver due to cirrhosis. But receiving a new liver comes with an exhausting daily routine of therapy to support the new liver to prevent rejection of the organ, and, also, to sustain life in the recipient. It's not a practical solution for the average PKU patient.

We are only 1 in 20,000, but we are out there.

One never knows, when simply passing by someone, or meeting someone, or even talking with them, what personal battles someone may be waging. Or what cross they have been called to carry.

Unless they share it with you.

There are far more potentially devasting and difficult-to-manage conditions than Phenylketonuria. But those of us who have PKU, we are out there. Our family always knows. And our friends may think that we eat weird. And that we have to drink special drinks all the time. But deep down, do they really know what PKU is?

Those who have PKU are a rare breed, yes, but people of all races, nationalities and creeds are tested for PKU.

You were tested.

In the 1970's, the routine testing of babies for the recessive PKU gene was started, and I was one of the first babies to be tested for the condition. Shortly after my birth, my parents received the news, and their reaction was probably like any other parents – of questioning.

Of anxiety.

Eventually, our family became a model of how PKU should be managed.

As we sat in the PKU specialist's office when I was still a boy, the doctor finished his exam and straightened his posture. He pushed his glasses up the ridge of his nose and looked at me with wide eyes. "You really are a phenomenon, Andrew. Your parents have been doing an excellent job with your diet, and you have become our star PKU child, Andrew."

My mother sat in the chair next to the examination table, beaming.

The doctor looked at her and nodded, and then back over to me, as I looked up at him, watching him tower over me, folding his binder, as he turned and placed it on the side counter. "Of course, we have discussed this with your mother already, but because your phenylalanine levels have been so good, we want to bring you to the Medical school to speak to the new doctors."

My mouth dropped open and I gasped. "Talk to the doctors?!"

My mother stood and looked at me. "They need to hear about everything directly from you, Andrew."

The doctor cleared his throat, and my mother looked back at him.

His arms were clasped at his waist. "The doctors need to know how you manage your PKU on a daily basis, Andrew. And your mom and dad play a

182

big role in that, but so do you. And they need to hear from *you*."

As we left the clinic later, and as I helped my mother carry the small boxes of Phenyl-Free formula into the back of the car, I fired questions at her, wondering what I should do and what I should say.

Decades later, when writing this book, I touched on the topic of being the PKU poster child, once again.

"You are a poster child, Andrew. You truly are. A success story. Keep that in mind, all the time."

I paused and set my beer down on the small table next to me, as the rocking chair halted. "That's what you both have told me, Dad."

I listened, holding the phone close to my ear, as he continued. "Andrew, you have to understand. Everything that we did when you were a little boy was an experiment. We had no idea if it would work or not. But you are one of the first PKU children to be placed on the diet, and even though I wasn't always there, I knew that your mother was doing her best to raise you the best way we knew how, which had no background. There was no manual for this. It was all a 'let's see if this works' type of situation. Not enough people had been put on your diet at that point, Andrew. You have to realize, this was the mid 1970's. Babies who were born just a few years before you had a very different outcome. We never knew if you would even develop normally."

"Mom has said that also," I said, taking a sip of my beer. I shifted my phone to my other ear. "And do you know, Dad? Do you know anything about mom breast feeding me? Mom was saying that the doctors didn't recommend doing it."

"No, no, of course they didn't. The breast milk had protein. But I remember what your mother did. She used to take a breast pump and set the milk aside and freeze it so it could be measured out for you. She then mixed it with your PKU formula."

"And the doctors said it couldn't be measured? When I was a baby?"

"Of course. They didn't know. And they didn't think of any alternative solutions."

Could that have made the difference?

I had always thought I was a fairly normal little boy. At least as normal as one could be as a boy, it seemed. I did all of the things that little boys do; I played cars, I watched cartoons, I played outside until my mom called for me from the back door to come inside as the sun sank below the horizon.

Yet, looking back, I can see how distinctly different I was.

I was the small boy, perhaps five years old, who sat in the middle of the dark blue carpeting in the aisle of the Catholic church my family went to during that time.

I sat in the center of a circle of tall adults; they were my mother's friends from the church.

I looked up at them as they looked down at me and then over at my mother. They seemed amused that I sat in the center of the circle, on the floor, looking up at them, as if I knew what they were thinking.

Wide eyes, that told a story. They knew, everyone knew, and I would know as I matured into an adult.

"Andrew is going to do something," one of the prayer members said.

My mother looked down at me, and smiled warmly, as only a mother could down when gazing down at her little boy. "He is destined for something special. Important."

I don't always know how much truth there was to that observation offered to my mother, but the story of me sitting in front of the prayer group members, after the church services had ended, became a story to discuss amongst family and friends in subsequent decades.

"There is just something about Andrew," some would say. "He is very special little boy, honey. And I can tell you that. And I know."

$$\mathscr{L}$$

I loved music, I played in the marching band, I hung out with my neighborhood friends, and I played with Matchbox cars. I played with my brother and sister in the back woods building forts, drinking lemonade, and playing army. I even played soccer.

There wasn't much about me that seemed different, in my perspective.

For me, all of the nuances of having a brain-threatening metabolic disorder diagnosed at birth, which include a protein restricted diet for life, regular blood tests, weekly visits to the doctors, bi-annual visits to the specialist, and taking home dozens of cases of a powered supplement formula which provided my body with the protein it needs, without the element that I was severely allergic to, seemed perfectly normal to me.

Was it?

I was never sure, at least not now, as I write this, a man who someone, in some way, made it to middle-age, without the ravages I was told would happen if I didn't follow my protein-restricted diet, and drink my powered formula (it was foul-smelling, I loathed it) exactly.

Somehow, I managed to make it close to fifty years of age.

I graduated with honors, Cum Laude no less, from a prestigious university in Philadelphia. And then I would be destined to write – and publish – over a dozen novels, which have received positive reviews. And I was destined to win an award for writing Supernatural fiction, the Gold Medal, no less, for writing the best novel of the year for the International Book Awards by Readers' Favorite.

No one with Phenylketonuria could achieve something like that, it seemed.

Right?

Could they?

Would it be possible?

Regardless of how special my mother, or my family, or any friends, believed me to be, that destiny simply seemed unreachable for someone dealing with a metabolic disorder that crept into my life on a regular basis, even as an adult.

Right? Did I have a more difficult journey, or a heavier cross, or more steps to take than anyone else did? I don't really think so. Many others have heavier crosses and more complicated journeys than I do. This is simply my own puzzle, and putting everything together, and finding that picture.

Phenylketonuria was little-known and scarcely studied when I was born. Yet it was known enough to have developed a test, and that is one of the things that saved my life.

But in those days, they had a test.

Everyone is tested for PKU at birth.

You were. Do you remember that? Do you remember it being mentioned earlier in this book?

Probably not. But you would know if you had it.

And the reason you were tested is for the same uncertainties that I was faced with throughout my life. PKU is a relentless, unforgiving, and ravaging metabolic disorder. It's not like the typical food allergy. My throat doesn't close when I eat something that my body can't have, something that my liver cannot process because it's missing the enzyme to break down the protein products into the amino acids which the body can absorb.

PKU comes like a thief in the night when I eat something I shouldn't have.

The phenylalanine, which is present in most foods, builds up in my bloodstream, because my liver cannot break it down. I don't have immediate symptoms, and I likely never will.

But there are symptoms.

It's not like IBS; I don't have to run to the bathroom. I don't break out in hives, or rashes, at least not initially. When I eat something that I shouldn't have, my body quietly digests it as if everything was normal. I feel nourished with a burst of energy just as I would if I was eating properly, and I go on about my day.

The veiled sense of normalcy can cause a laissez-faire attitude towards the PKU diet. I can eat anything, I would think. The doctors don't know what they are talking about, I will tell myself again.

My mother is taking this too seriously.

The thoughts would clatter through my mind, making me doubt that the PKU diet was even *necessary* because when I would eat what "they" told me not to, nothing would happen.

I didn't carry an EpiPen.

There was no reason to.

I got into thinking that, maybe, just maybe, everything around me was misguided. The world was wrong. I was being told to eat a certain way and drink a foul-tasting and smelling medical supplementary drink to get my protein — when it tasted *so much better* to take it in while eating the "forbidden foods."

I dodged a bullet.

One that could have had devastating effects on my life. The reason why both you and I were tested for PKU at birth is because of the horrendous effects of the condition, not only on the central nervous system, but, most importantly, the brain.

And the mind.

Oh, my mind.

In those days, in the days when I was a little older and finding myself more under my own watchful protection, I found myself exploring the different foods, when I wasn't under the eye of my mother, or my father, or my family. I started to experiment.

I dealt with a mind that could not focus.

You may be reading this, thinking, there are many of us who have difficulty focusing. Those who have ADHD are common, and there are medications to alleviate the condition.

What is the deal with PKU?

Why is it so ravaging on the mind? Why the restricted diet? And the frequent blood tests? What was the purpose of the scrutiny?

Looking back, when I thought of the days when I was a child, and when I didn't fully understand *why* my mother was restricting what I ate, and *why* my father took me to a doctor's office in a neighboring state to have my blood drawn with a needle from my arm in a green-top tube.

Why did they do it?

My father took me to my doctor's appointments two states away to have my blood tested, which would be mailed back to my home state during my summer visits. I knew that they were my parents, and I listened to them.

It was always how it had been.

191

Yet still, I questioned all who were in my life placing restrictions on me.

In my rebellious days, while in high school, I experienced, for the first time, the effects of the high levels of blood phenylalanine in my body.

$$\mathscr{L}$$

When my father took me for those blood tests, it was to check the levels of phenylalanine in my blood, just as with the days with my mother. When I was a teenager, I didn't care about the levels of the phenylalanine.

I simply wanted to fit in with the others.

I didn't want to be different.

I didn't want to be special. I simply wanted to go through life blending in with others.

I didn't want to go out to eat at a restaurant, because the spotlight would shine on me while we sat at the table, looking at the menus.

My father would stare at the menu, shaking his head. "There's nothing here for Andrew," he would say. "Not even a salad."

Those were the days before when eating differently was trendy.

It was the time when I simply wanted to fit in, and restaurants wanted to stick to the menu; I wanted to be liked, and listened to, and cared about, and have friends who enjoyed being friends with me. I wanted to go out to eat with family and there not be a fuss about what I was going to have to eat.

As the years progressed, my feelings remained the same.

When I entered high school, I was still like that same, inquisitive little boy, wanting others to like me. At that point, my mother had already collected a box full of construction paper and macaroni artwork I made when I was in middle school.

But in high school, it was time for me to truly perform.

The time had come to start cultivating the mind, developing it for adulthood, yet, I was presented with a unique challenge of which I was entirely unaware. There came the period when I didn't think that the others knew what they were talking about.

193

I was questioning my diet, and the reasoning for it, and I was actively experimenting with things that I shouldn't be. And that was when I was teetering on the edge of disaster.

LL

During the high school years when the first period of lunch was always at ten o'clock in the morning, I found it to be bizarre. Yet, by the time the early lunch period arrived, I could feel the rumbling in my stomach.

"You must not starve yourself," the dietician had told me at my most recent visit with the PKU specialist. "Your body protein will break down if you become hungry for too long of a time. And your blood levels will go up."

"Even if I don't cheat and eat the wrong things?"

She nodded. "Even if you don't cheat."

She opened the large, red binder. I watched her as she flipped through the pages. "But Andrew, you have been cheating, haven't you?"

I shook my head nervously. "I don't think so," I stammered. "I probably go too long without eating, like you said." I looked over at my mother, who sat in the opposite chair, against the wall, as I sat with the dietician. I could feel my underarms and palms get damp as my face grow hot.

My mother said nothing but looked over at me as she raised her eyebrows, tilting her head to the side.

I shifted in my chair, returning my focus to the dietician. She was slowly turning pages in the large, red binder, looking down. I shifted in my chair. "No, no," I said. "I am not a cheater. Haven't been doing it."

The dietician didn't reply, but merely flipped through the pages, studying them. After a few minutes, she looked over at me. "These levels, Andrew. They're up and down. It's very strange." She closed the book and looked at me directly in the eyes.

I could feel my heart pounding.

"Andrew, these types of fluctuations are larger than a little bit of your body protein breaking down. What about the chicken leg?"

I froze.

My head snapped over to my left and I glared at my mother.

My eyes became wide, pleading, as my heart pounded in my chest. My face shifted, hot, red, saying *why did you tell her about that?*

She folded her arms and leaned back into her chair.

I slowly returned my attention to the dietician as she looked up and put her glasses on the front of her head, nestled in her hair. "Andrew, this level is 27. You need to get your phenylalanine level down to between 6 and 8. You will be able to concentrate better, all sorts of things."

"Your anxiety won't be so bad," my mother offered.

I took a slow, deep breath, and sighed. "Mom!"

I had been caught.

They found me out.

No matter how much I attempted to conceal it, the evidence always seemed to appear. And no matter how many times I was lectured and was told that cheating was destroying my mind and my body, I continued to do it, for in my high school years, I wanted so desperately to fit in with everyone else. I craved similarity, and a connection, and I didn't care what the repercussions could be.

Time had passed since I had helped myself to that chicken leg in the small drawer in the refrigerator. I had thought no one would notice. The day I sampled it was years before high school, and I was still a young boy. I had been following my diet as best as I could, but curiosity took over. And then, it happened.

I tasted glory.

What I had been missing all along.

As I carefully placed the bone in the same baggie that my mom had stored the leg in, I shoved it in my pocket and headed upstairs. *This seems to be perfectly fine*, I thought. *They don't seem to know what they are talking about. I feel just fine. Why do I have to avoid this? It tastes so good!*

I crouched down next to my bed and saw the multitude of old shoe boxes underneath the frame, and I slowly parted two of them. As I pulled out the small baggie, I looked at the bone.

No one will know. What they don't know won't hurt them.

But it would hurt me.

And they knew. For the missing chicken leg in the refrigerator was noted, and my room was the first to be searched.

CHAPTER NINE

I have never been one to hold grudges.

There have been times that I have been upset with people in my life, but it rarely lasts very long at all.

There is something inside of me that makes me want people to be happy with me.

I want them to be proud of me, to like what I am doing, and to remember me fondly, especially those who are close to me in my life, particularly my friends and family.

As my mom and I loaded up dozens of small cardboard boxes, packed with the white and blue cans of the phenyl-free powder, I watched as we got inside the car. As she slowly pulled away from the Porte cochere outside the front of the Hospital, I looked over at her as she navigated the crowded streets.

"I remember you said that at Rutgers, when we were in front of the auditorium of doctors," I said, finally, breaking the silence. "About the chicken leg."

I watched as she continued looking ahead, watching the road. "And I remember you poking my side as I was speaking."

I scoffed as I stared out the window, watching the activity on the side of the thoroughfare, as the city gave way to inner suburbs. "Well, I was only ten."

"People need to know, Andrew. Especially the doctors. When you cheat, your mind is at risk. It shows up on your skin. And your attitude. I brought up the chicken leg also so the students could see that you can recover from the cheating too."

I leaned my head back on the headrest, closed my eyes, and thought about the day in the Rutgers auditorium when mom had told a legion of doctors that I had eaten a chicken leg at ten years old.

The gasp had startled me.

The doctors were medical students at Rutgers University, all seeking to learn more about this mysterious condition called Phenylketonuria. But they knew enough, not only about the diet and the consequences of cheating, but also about the necessity of the treatment diet to warrant such a gasp, which had given me pause, despite being a young boy. I remember writing my daily diet list and their measurements on the chalkboard in the lower presentation area of the sprawling auditorium, telling them that if I wanted a hot dog to similar gasps.

I explained them that I would need to eat very low protein foods – such as salads and fruit – for the time leading up to the consumption of a hot dog, and then, also, have the same low-protein foods afterwards. I am unsure, to this day, if the doctors accepted my reasoning for having a hot dog.

My eyes opened as the car went over a bump. "I'm really sick and tired of everyone always assuming that my level is high, mom."

"You have to be honest, Andrew," mom said. "When we are in the clinic, when your dietician examines your history, she knows when you have been cheating. It isn't something that you can hide, Andrew."

"But I'm not *always* cheating! Sometimes I get upset about something."

I lowered my chin, sulking in my seat.

201

I looked over at my mom as she pulled the car into the driveway, as she turned the car around, and started backing it close to the garage door. As she cut the engine, I got out and opened the back of the station wagon and started to unload the boxes of my formula into the garage. "You know, sometimes I wonder if all this is even necessary. I can't even tell a difference."

"We all can tell a difference when your level is high."

I stacked the boxes in the corner and let out an exasperated sigh. I shook my head. "You know, mom, I am sick and tired of PKU being used as a scapegoat for emotions! I do get upset. *Just like everyone else!*"

"Of course, you do," mom said. "But we all can tell when you've been cheating. You become a different person."

I shook my head as we went inside.

As I headed up the stairs to my room, I flung myself on the bed, shortly followed by my loyal black dog Inky.

We rescued her from a farm, and we never really knew what breed she was, but always suspected she was at least part Labrador. She jumped up next to me and curled up next to me as I lay on my stomach, my arms crossed, my chin resting on my arms.

Nothing made sense to me.

I was in high school now; I was finally finding some friends; I had a cafeteria full of food that seemed just perfectly fine to me. Sure, I got upset. I became irritable. But how many times would I have to explain to my mother that, sometimes, I am simply upset about something?

I eased myself up on my elbows and looked over at Inky. She raised her head and looked up at me with her big, brown, loving eyes. I started to pet her head. "I just want to be normal," I said.

And I lowered my chin back on my arms again and listened to the late summer rain which started to fall. Certainly, there would be someone who would understand my logic. Why was there such a fuss when I seemed fine, even better, when I ate the foods that I liked to experiment with? Little did I know, I was walking around completely oblivious to the downward spiral I was on.

The alarm clock tore me out of my dream world, and I opened my eyes slowly, reaching up and feeling the sandy grit in my eyes.

My head felt stuffy.

And I saw Inky still sleeping at my feet, curled in a ball. It was those early High School mornings which I have never remembered fondly. They were always hazy. They were always muted; yet I always found myself to be on time.

The mornings were too early.

My mother had always told me that I was an early morning baby. I was awake and boisterous by six thirty, regardless of what time I settled down the night before. But this morning was different. The sun wasn't even up.

I swung my legs out of the bed and flung the sheet off of me, hanging my head down in my stuffiness. I got up, as Inky raised her head slowly and looked up at me, as if to wonder why we were rising so early. I pandered over to the bathroom, twisted the knob to turn on the water, and once I got in, I relished the warm water, washing the sleep away slowly.

I rubbed the shampoo through my hair, leaned my head on the side of the shower, and just stood, my eyes closed. I could still feel that sleep had its grip on me; I could feel dreams streaming into my mind even though I was standing up, and I just needed a few. More. Minutes.

"That's what I do," I said the following weekend when we were sitting together at the local lake on Saturday afternoon, talking about how much we hated rising so early in the morning. "Once the shampoo is all lathered up in my hair, I let it sit and lean my head on the wall."

My sister looked up at me, tilting her head to the side, as my older brother stripped his shirt off, and headed straight into the water as delicate waves lapped at the shore.

"The shampoo needs some time to work," I said, looking over at my sister, who removed her sunglasses and looked at me, raising her eyebrows. "I am three years younger than you, Andrew. And I am old enough to know that you are feeding me bullshit."

We both changed our focus as Mom emerged from the lake with a large raft, a huge smile across her face. "I heard you guys," she said. And then she looked down at me, as she grabbed a towel and started to dry herself off. "You've always been an early riser, Andrew. Since you were a baby. What happened?"

I folded my arms and looked out at the lake and the swimmers in the bright sun as the trees caught the wind above then. I watched as other children practiced their diving on the long, rickety dock, and huffed and puffed. "I can't do that anymore. Those early mornings don't agree with me."

It didn't make sense to me until decades later, while researching this book.

In my high school years, which were my primary cheating years, my blood levels were running high. Too much protein, no means to break it down, and the level of toxin in my body, mainly phenylalanine, was too high. No matter how much I tried to plead that my irritability was caused by "basic human emotion", and my skin conditions, such as eczema, was caused by allergy season, the blood tests would reveal the truth, and they always did.

Waking up for school in those days took great effort, and I also remember falling asleep, frequently, as early as 8pm each night, claiming I was too exhausted to stay up to a more reasonable hour because I woke up so early to go to high school.

A teenager, exhausted, all the time.

Now I know.

Elevated blood phenylalanine levels can cause fatigue. That also helps me manage my protein intake as a PKU adult, as I know if I have periods of low energy, and sleepiness, and exhaustion.

These symptoms, fatigue, irritability, and skin conditions, were the tamest. And I was lucky to have experienced only them, for the most part.

But there are other symptoms that could have had a far more devasting effect on my life.

My attention span would continue to suffer, causing a failure to thrive; my judgment could have been affected and may have been, causing me to make poor decisions potentially leading to consequences; I could have had a seizure or worse.

My sister knew I was feeding her bullshit, and I was.

Yet, there was something about my mindset in those years. I knew I was lying to my family, despite believing the lies I told.

Everyone knew I was cheating. It was written in my actions, I felt the sleepiness, yet didn't make the connection.

They all knew, except me, it seems. Maybe I was simply going through a rebellious phase. Maybe I didn't think that the diet was even necessary, that the doctors and my family were lying to *me* all along.

But I continued my narrative in those years.

My mood swings, skin problems, and sleepiness were not a result of my cheating. That is what I insisted on.

But everyone knew.

I could make as many arguments as people would listen to, but the bloodwork would not lie. And everyone knew I was struggling with the diet.

Except me.

I thought the diet was a bunch of unnecessary bullshit.

Or did I?

L

I could feel the gnaw in my stomach as I stood in line in the cafeteria. I knew what I was about to do. It was undeniably premeditated, but I didn't care.

I held my two dollars in my right hand and shifted back and forth from foot to foot. I looked down at the crumbled bills in my hands; they were wet, and so were my palms.

Today was hoagie day.

I was following my diet. I had been getting salads almost every day; but I saw the sandwiches on the top of the lunch line, wrapped in clear plastic wrap, stacked neatly like soldiers. I wished that I could try them. *Just one bite…*I thought. *Just a single bite. I only want to find out what it tastes like…*

The buns were loaded with all the things I was told not to eat. Ham, salami, pastrami, provolone…there they all were. As I stood in the line, waiting, carrying my small, plastic tray, I waited as the students in front of me laughed boisterously. As they moved around, back and forth, it revealed the salads, sitting on ice under the plastic sneeze guard.

My palms still felt wet.

Cheating was not always planned and calculated; sometimes, I would see something and know that it would be a poor decision, but in that moment of temptation, I would sometimes be unable to control myself.

This time, however, I planned to cheat.

I wanted to taste the sandwich.

Everyone in my life cared for my mind, and how it developed. But I just had to try everything. I had to taste the tastes.

Feel the texture and the flavors.

Everything seems just fine, I thought, as I passed the salads, and slowly reached out and picked up on of the neatly wrapped Italian Hoagies. I picked it up, feeling its softness and heaviness in my hand, and slowly placed it on the lunch tray.

The guilt immediately set in.

Mom was a single parent.

She worked hard for the money, and was giving it to me, in confidence. And most of the time, I did. But this time, I just had to try it. She knew I was experimenting, without me having to tell her.

But then, I did not have the same thoughts as I do now, decades later. My family worked tirelessly to make me a successful person, and by picking up that hoagie filled with meats, cheeses, and far more phenylalanine than my poor body could handle, I made my choice. It was the ultimate level of disrespect.

In my high school days, I just wanted to fit in. I wanted to find out what I was missing. I no longer wanted to be the strange kid who sat and ate a daily salad.

I wanted to eat what the other students were eating.

When I pulled the two dollar bills I had shoved into my pocket when I had grabbed the tray, which my mother had given me, entrusting me to make the right choices, I used that money, which my mother gave to me, as a single parent who struggled with the bills, to pay for a sandwich that I should never have been having.

It was a sandwich that would cause me to become irritable, and unable to focus. It would cause my skin to break out in eczema, because my body had no way to process the incoming protein overload, and there was no other way for my body to rid itself of the toxins. And I would be sleepy every day.

"Andrew, have you been cheating again?"

I stopped scratching my inner foot and looked up. My mother stood above me, as I sat on the couch. I had taken off one of my socks and started scratching my inner foot, which was bubbled up in a fiery red rash.

"Your skin has been pretty bad lately."

"It's fine, mom."

She sighed. "I got you some more of those acne pads you can rub on your cheeks to help clean your skin."

She knew.

So did my brother and sister. I don't know if my father knew the extent of my cheating, as, in those days, my parents had already gotten divorced.

I was also spending two months every summer in another state with him and my step siblings, and although no specific episodes of cheating stuck out in my mind when I was there. I am certain I found ways to experiment with food, and so I would imagine he knew also.

It was only me that was in denial.

I looked at the wadded dollar bills as I slowly handed them over to the lunch lady. I raised my head, gradually, and she looked at me, with a big smile on her face. "Enjoy!"

I smiled wanly and nodded, turning toward the sea of crowded tables in the cafeteria.

The tables were packed, and the chatter filled the room.

Lunch was always exciting.

Students ran and teachers told them to slow down and walk carefully. Kids laughed at the round lunch tables.

And then the familiar and cheerful voice of my Algebra teacher shocked me back to reality. "Oh look! A *hah-gie*!"

I froze.

I slowly lowered my head, looking down at the hoagie I wasn't supposed to have. I turned to face her, and she was smiling and pointed at my sandwich. "That looks great, Andrew!"

All I could do was hang my head as my cheeks grew hot.

I'd been found out.

I wasn't supposed to eat this, and I knew it.

But she didn't know about my PKU. So why would she question me at all? My tray looked just like all of the others. I was having a hoagie too. And I seemed perfectly in place. I turned back to face the sea of students at the round tables ahead of me. No one knew. I could sit at any one of those tables, start eating my meat-and-cheese-filled sandwich, and no one would think anything of it. I would blend in with the others; I wouldn't be the weird kid who ate salads and

213

fruit every day. I would be eating the same foods that they were.

And somehow, I felt that it earned me a rite of passage.

I didn't think that I was doing any harm to my body; each bite was wonderful, and delicious, and made me food good. It was filling far beyond anything I had eaten.

I may have thought that I got away with it.

When I sat at the lunch table, I said hello to several of the other students who I had been slowly making friends with and placed my tray on the table. They were laughing and involved in their own conversation. And when I looked at them, chatting and taking bites from their own hoagies, I then looked down at my tray.

My food looked exactly the same.

I knew my tray was *supposed* to look different.

I knew that I *should* be fielding questions from the other students, as they would ask me why I wasn't eating the same food they were.

But today, it was the same food. I had a meat and cheese filled hoagie, and I stared at it, sitting and waiting. My sinful creation.

"What are you doing, Andrew? Are you going to eat your lunch?"

I snapped out of my musings.

I looked up and over at them and nodded. "Yeah, yeah. I was just…waiting, you know?"

They shook their heads and laughed.

"We don't have much more time! You have to tell us about *Backdraft* again." And then they giggled.

But I wasn't listening to them.

Of course, they were poking fun at the movie I watched and talked about incessantly. That and *Bram Stoker's Dracula*.

I didn't hear them, and I didn't care about the movies at that moment. I was staring at my hoagie, hesitating, waiting for some form of approval to eat that I never would receive.

Don't do it, Andrew.

Don't do it. Don't do it. Don't do it.

I picked up the sandwich and drew it close to my mouth. I could smell the sweetness of the peppers and lettuce and the earthy spiciness of the meats.

I took a small breath and exhaled.

And took a bite.

I ignored the shadows which fought through my mind because I didn't care.

This felt and tasted *too fucking good.*

I started to devour the sandwich, lost in the cavernous beauty of the taste of the prohibited. They told me no, and I was saying yes. I didn't care. I was living in that moment, loving the taste, the mouthfeel, everything.

It was so. Damn. Good.

Those three pestering letters that always seemed to make their presence known at the most inopportune times were shoveled away, far from my thoughts, as I chewed, basking in the glory of the forbidden, and then I swallowed.

Dear Andrew,

Oh, are we going to have some fun with you…

With regards,

Demon one, Demon two, and Demon three.

I was in a massive state of denial.

But I was lying to myself.

My skin broke out and I suffered from recurrent eczema during those years. My mother knew what I was doing, but perhaps not to the extent. I was rebelling against the diet, against everything; questioning if it was even necessary and protesting any form of difference. I had grown tired of the restrictions, and although I felt the consequences of my choices were minor, there were others in my life who knew what was going on, and what could happen if I continued the path of self-destruction.

I continued with the lie, but the truth always comes out.

And it did.

These days, I still wonder why the anxiety sets in. Although I am not actively cheating now like I was in high school, I have learned to listen to my body over the years. Even though I still track what I eat on a day-to-day basis like I always have, I do not write everything down and measure out the portions like my parents did when I was a child. Still, there are days in recent times, when I knew I'd had too much.

Or too little.

It was during the days when I fell off the high wire; I got the balance wrong.

Either I would be eating too much of the food that I was able to have, which would cause a buildup of too much protein, or I would not be eating enough food altogether. In that case, my own body protein would start to break down, nourishing my body, yes, but also raising my blood phenylalanine levels just the same, which causes the exact same effects as if I had been blatantly cheating.

Even so, whenever that would happen, even as a middle-aged man, the resulting symptoms of high blood phenylalanine would always appear, usually a day or two later. I might become irritable or "mad at the world", seemingly for no apparent reason. Almost always, my anxiety level would increase, significantly, sometimes to the point of being debilitating.

Why do I have these same old fears?

I would never be able to answer the question; I would simply have to get back on the horse and continue forward. As an author, many writing days have been lost due to over indulgence, or, not eating enough, as the clutches of deep anxiety would thread itself into my veins, tying the ropes around me, keeping me from doing anything aside from lying in bed, wishing the demons in my head would quiet.

It's not what I could even attempt to control.

It wasn't the purpose of acceptance, or maybe it was. As the many clocks kept ringing within my mind, multiple alarms and tick-ticks I could feel my heart as it beats inside my chest.

Another sleepless night.

There was something about the night. The unknown and the uncertainty of the darkness. What I could not see; what I was unable to control. I didn't know why the feelings set in. I never had a fingernail biting habit, but I might as well have. I should have known this when I was younger, when I was awake, my bed next to the window, sitting up, looking outside in the darkness.

Terrified.

What could it have been?

Why didn't I know?

Of course, I was deep in the throes.

For someone who suffers from anxiety, it's the period of relief that we desire, when the realization comes that there is nothing really to worry about. But until we get there, the darkness remains real and tightens its grip. I craved liberation without knowing that I wanted to taste the sweetness of release. It was the dark masterpiece of my own creation; I weaved the plot, and composed my own symphony of strain, and I was in the chorus of despair.

Was I simply caught in the crossfire?

I was a little bit hazy. I didn't know then why I was suffering from the ramifications of the disagreement of sorts; the levels of phenylalanine in my blood had become increasingly toxic from an influx of the forbidden. There was nowhere it could go as it built in my blood.

I could not shine with the battle waging within; my mind at war with my body, my body screaming for and there was nothing else I could do but endure the consequences of my choices. Sometimes, I didn't even know what I was worrying about. They say destiny lies in the stars, as I looked upwards, I wondered.

What was I destined to become?

L

And then I suddenly looked in the mirror and saw a forty-year-old man staring back at me in the reflection.

My eyes were red, my hair was wet, and I stared directly at myself with an intensity I can only remember

I wrapped the towel around me, taking the second towel which I always grabbed and placed it around my shoulders.

I looked up at my reflection. I am an adult now. I should not have these same problems.

But I did.

When it came to food, I still wanted to fit in. I could see the bags starting to form under my eyes, the lines. "Stop doing this."

Stop doing what?

I inhaled sharply through my nostrils and looked at my reflection. "Stop being a fucking *fake*!"

You are young. Still beautiful. There is still hope for you. You still have a body, don't you?

221

I slammed my hands down on the counter. "I don't have the body!"

You should have a body. We all do.

I looked at myself directly in the mirror, reached up, and wiped away the steam. "You have to stop cheating."

My eyes were red, rimming with tears, as they streamed down my cheeks. I reached up and wiped the mirror with a hand towel. "You have to stop. I can't keep going on like this. You are destroying your mind. You are destroying your *body*."

Why did it take so long to have this chat with myself?

I had always been told, and I had known, that my actions would be detrimental to any type of life growth. It seemed like I was still on a path seeking acceptance, not only that but love. I knew my family loved me. But I wanted the world to love me. I was born a people pleaser, and it was tough to please anyone, it seemed. I felt some of my talents could be a curse, and then I stopped.

I was not actively cheating.

But you are destroying your body. In one way, or another.

"This is not high school."

I reached up and cleared the mist from the mirror once again. My eyes were piercing yet pained. "I am not destroying my mind. I have to find my inspiration. I am a writer. I want to be an author."

You're already an author, you stupid fuck. Pretty soon, you'll be planted. Time to shit or get off the pot.

I didn't want to face those demons any longer, but I knew they weren't going anywhere.

Why was my creativity fueled by despair? But I asked myself the question.

"Why did it take so long for you to come to this revelation?"

I knew, deep within myself, that any turn towards alcohol would not bring me to where I wanted to go. At that point in my life, I was building my career as an author, and I told others that creative fuel was important.

And maybe it was.

We creative people must find inspiration somewhere.

Still, I had my three letters to consider.

My PKU; my missing liver enzyme.

And so, everything must be counted. While I may have had difficult chats in the mirror with myself after showers, I knew, deep within my mind, that the only person that could change me, and get me to that next stepping stone, was me.

Sometimes tough conversations must be had. And sometimes, it needs to be you having that tough conversation with yourself.

CHAPTER TEN

I am almost forty as I am writing this now.

When I look back on my adult life, my childhood seems so distantly away. But it's my childhood that I really have been needing to pay attention to. You see, it was my mother who paid strict attention to what I was, and was not, able to eat, having Phenylketonuria.

Still, I will always remember the lancet. That sinister, tiny sword, with an appetite for blood.

That small, reflective, shiny, pointed inch-long sliver of steel that always caught the light when my eyes widened with terror. It looked like a tiny arrow, perhaps a dagger. In the shape of a sword.

The sharp point on one end, leading to a rectangular tail, squared off opposite the point. But its shape didn't really matter, for it only had one mission, and one mission only: to jab into my finger.

Pierce the skin. Draw blood.

Causing me to cry out in pain; for my heart to pound, and my eyes to widen with terror as I would plead with my mother to skip the blood test that week.

But she knew she couldn't skip it.

She never did; no matter how much I cried, no matter how much I pleaded.

No matter how much pain the jab of the lancet would cause; no matter how loud my protesting became, as we would sit on the cool tile of the bathroom floor; she sat, her legs open, me sitting, her little boy, her little Andrew, on my knees, on the floor between her legs, holding my finger up in front of her.

She held my small hand, and then I would pull it away from her. The striking smell of alcohol caused my muscles to get tense, and the anxiety to set in.

It still does.

That smell always led to the jab.

It was a dreaded day that came too often when I was a little boy, and I knew that my mother absolutely hated causing pain to her son…but she knew, no matter how much it hurt her to hurt me, that it was something that had to happen.

There was no other way to check my blood. It was to see if I had been following my diet correctly, eating the right food, in the correct amounts, at the proper times.

For what I had, my "PKU" as the doctors called it, and the Phenylketonuria, as the medical journals called it, was so extraordinarily rare when I was diagnosed with it, that very little was known how to even *monitor* it and see if the intervention measures were successful.

And it hurt my mother to see me in pain, but it was a necessary thing, seeing the light catch that lancet. I froze and watched as she held it, grasping it between her thumb and index finger.

I didn't really know what was going through her mind when the point jabbed into my thumb.

I screamed and cried and wailed, as she hastily pressed my thumb on the small test circles on the test form.

I didn't know what she was thinking about. As a young boy, that is. Now, as an adult, I can only imagine how it must have felt to hurt one's child. To hear the cries of pain, even if it was for a good purpose and a needed thing.

The blood testing had become a weekly routine, and sometimes even more often if my levels were running high. But in high school, there had to be a solution, or those school cafeteria days of eating hoagies, and other high-protein foods, which my body was unable to process, would undo what she and my family had worked so hard to ensure – the formation of my mind.

And the cheating had to stop.

The chicken leg and the hoagie seemed simple, harmless, and nourishing.

Yet, in those years, when I was enamored with what I was told was forbidden, my mind was on the cusp of destruction, without my even knowing it.

I had to do something, but in those years, I wasn't aware that there was even a problem.

When I was in high school, several of the classes that I took as electives, and while I did not know it at the time, these classes had prepared me for my future as an artist, and a writer.

Had I continued the path of eating different foods that I found delicious, and eternally tempting, then I most certainly would have wound up like one of my mother's mentally challenged clients; I would have required assistance for the remainder of my life.

I would not have achieved the level of success that I have.

There would be no books.

I would never have painted canvases or dressed in character costumes while exploring the inspiration for characters that I have created in my novels.

I would never have produced videos which explore the origins of my art, or haunted locations, or would have become an entertainer.

My entire life would have been a struggle, of a different kind, depending on how much cheating I would have done.

It would be as if I were living in an alternate reality.

Had I continued the path I was on in high school, I very well may have wound up in assisted living at a very young age.

Perhaps I would have wound up in jail. Or worse. I don't know how long my mind and central nervous system would have been able to tolerate the elevation of blood phenylalanine levels, and how long

I would be able to remain a productive person who didn't require regular assistance.

I wasn't thinking about that while I was in high school in the cafeteria.

I simply wanted to fit in and try the foods that were on the forbidden list throughout my life, because when I ate them, I felt good. I didn't have any type of horrendous reaction; they tasted amazing.

They tasted like life.

And my PKU always faded away when I was cheating, if only for a moment. It was no longer there. I was able to place it in the background, take it out of my body and shove it into my pocket for a bit.

This is what normal is, Andrew. Enjoy it while it lasts.

I was normal.

I felt normal.

This is what everybody else is eating, so why couldn't I? My throat never closed. I do not own an EpiPen. It was like the excitement of Christmas morning combined with the thrill of doing something I wasn't supposed to do. It was food I was always told I shouldn't eat.

And that made it taste *so damn good.*

And then, almost immediately after I took my last bite, the guilt set in.

I could see my family's faces in my mind, and picture how hard they all worked for me, fighting for the protection of my cognizance. I saw them navigating the rough seas of uncertainty, battling the setbacks, another of which I was creating.

I have learned that the consequences come like a thief in the night. There is no immediate reaction.

The subsequent erratic blood levels became the fallen fruit of my life; they were there, stained, and rotted. I didn't want them, but I knew that I must deal with them. I knew that I must partake of the rotten fruit if I wanted to grow.

For within the fruit there are many lessons.

ℒ

The classroom for my high school art class had several large worktables where the students sat together in small groups. There was something about art and creativity that captivated me then.

I stared at the pile of clay on the table in front of me.

We were supposed to sculpt something. I rested my chin in my hands as I looked at the small, grey mountain. Across the table, several of my classmates were hard at work molding their clay, dipping their hands in the water bowl, and rubbing the putty, grasping it and coaxing it into, what seemed to me, to be works of art.

I leaned back in my chair and sighed. Where was *my* talent?

I watched as my classmate molded his clay, easing his hands around the structure, as he raised his head and looked over at me. His eyes drifted downwards. "You haven't started?"

I shook my head slowly as he leaned forward, examining my pile of clay.

"You could always make an ashtray."

The girl next to him let out a chuckle.

"That's all I do in this class is make ashtrays," I said, pulling pieces of clay apart, and rubbing it in my palms, gradually forming it in a small sphere. "And no one in my family smokes."

The boy and girl erupted in laughter as I grinned at them.

I had an idea.

As I separated the clay into small, round balls, I picked one up and set it on the table. I eased my palm over it and started rolling. My face contorted as I concentrated on the putty, feeling it warm beneath my palm as I rolled; I watched as it fingered outwards into a long cylinder, as if it were a snake. Once I was satisfied, I stopped rolling and formed the cylinder of putty into a small circle.

The boy across the table formed a vase and he looked up, examining my work. "Are you making a vase too?"

I shrugged. "I'm just going with it. But maybe. Maybe for my mom. Maybe she could put some flowers in it."

He leaned forward and looked at the small clay ring.

"Well," he said. "You need a bottom to your vase." He pointed over to some excess clay. "Grab some of that. You can roll it out and knead it down to about a quarter inch or so. Then form it into a circle. That can be your bottom."

It made sense to me.

I looked down at the clay ring that I had formed, and wondered what I was doing, placing that ring together with no bottom. But as I grabbed a small glob of clay and started kneading and warming it on the table in front of me, I appreciated the help. I hadn't known that I was making a vase until he noticed it. There was something about my mind, something I still needed to harness.

As I molded the clay and formed the rings, I placed them on top of each other, as the vase slowly formed. I examined my handy work. This would be a perfect gift for my mother. As music started to waft towards the art room from a distance, I looked over at the others.

"It's the band," he said, as he prepped his vase for baking.

I turned my head towards the door, listening to the music. It wasn't perfect, nor was it grand.

But it spoke to me.

It called me closer, and I knew, then, that despite the curiosity that washed through me as I listened in the hallway, and I did not know at the time, but I was being pointed towards a much healthier, better direction. Little did I know that the arts would save me and give me something to focus on rather than the fear of being different and the many foods which were toxic to me in an effort to be like everyone else.

Perhaps it was time for me to start emerging from my shell; to being in the transformation from a caterpillar into a butterfly.

In those years, I had spent a lot of time and energy, in an attempt to prevent the world from discovering my deep, dark secret, which was PKU, taking extreme measures of deliberately ordering and eating foods that were forbidden for me in an effort to blend in.

I had to change my focus.

I wanted to keep the days secret when I caved to the temptations of the waiting forbidden foods in the refrigerator. Because I had developed a taste for them. In the days when I was in high school, I dealt with those temptations daily.

I would see my friends eating – and enjoying – foods that I was told I could not eat.

I was told if I ate them, that I would become brain damaged, and that I would have to live in a group home for the rest of my life, requiring assistance with basic activities and mental functions. In those days, when I was in high school surrounded by daily temptations and curiosities, I would stand in the kitchen and stare at the refrigerator.

My older brother was away at college, and my younger sister wasn't around when I stood in the kitchen, my arm outstretched, my hand wrapped around the cool handle. I closed my eyes and remembered the previous night.

Mom had baked chicken legs for her and my sister.

I remember sitting and staring at their plates.

For the most part, our plates were the same.

We all had a pile of bright green beans, which I loved, and still do. But that is where the similarities stopped. They had from-the-box macaroni and cheese, and I had my special-order, low-protein pasta. It was tasty; my mother boiled it for me, and I could eat almost as much of it as I wanted.

Sometimes she made it with red tomato sauce, which added to the protein content, and other times some butter and seasoning salt would do just fine. I remember my little sister putting some seasoning salt on her bright orange macaroni.

Maybe she wanted to be like her big brother or maybe it just may have tasted that damn good.

236

Because seasoning salt and macaroni is like a match made in heaven.

Next to my plate was always a small glass of the formula which I was required to drink daily, and in those days, I remember it being sickeningly sweet, too-thick-to-swallow, with memories of gagging, and the occasional lump sent me into a full-on panic. It was a white powder, of which I went home with cases of after my bi-annual clinic appointment with PKU specialists and dieticians.

It was mixed with water.

When I was a younger boy, my mother would shake it for me in shakers, and the scene would repeat itself. She continued to shake while I sat on a stool at the kitchen counter, scrutinizing her shaking abilities.

My mother always wanted me to be able to experience some different tastes of various foods, even if they were on the forbidden list, especially if I was quite curious.

The three glasses which sat on the counter in front of me were small jars, perhaps no more than six or eight ounces.

But to my wide little boy eyes, as I would rest my chin on the counter and watch mom shake the formula through the filter of the curved glasses and raised my head when she held the shaker above the first glass.

The cream-colored, thick liquid started filling the first glass and I looked up. "I can't drink *three*, Mom. I *can't*." But that was a common occurrence – saving it all for the end of the day.

She sighed.

"You haven't had your milk all day. Your body needs this every day. You don't want to end up like one of my clients, do you?"

I crossed my arms on the counter and rested my head over my hands, looking up, watching her pour my milk into the three small glasses, with sad, puppy dog eyes.

My mom folded her arms and looked down at me, her eyebrows raised.

My eyes widened as I looked up at her. "One of your *clients*?!"

Even at that tender young age, I knew about my mom's clients.

They weren't the type of clients an accountant or an attorney would have; my mother lived a life of service and caring for others. As a social worker, she spent her career being a paid angel for the state and was particularly adept at helping the developmentally disabled.

"*I am not a retard!*"

My mother gasped. "Andrew! Don't talk about them like that. *That is a mean word.* They are people just like you and me. Some of them could have had PKU – just like you – but they were born too early."

She placed one of the glasses of creamy liquid in front of me.

"You have to drink that, Andrew. If you don't want to wind up like one of my clients. They didn't have this type of help. You do."

I looked up at the darkened back hallway behind the kitchen and heard the approach of footsteps.

My aunt emerged, visiting from California, wearing a flowing, and flowery summer nightgown. Her glasses were tiny ovals in front of her eyes, and her bushy, red curly hair framed her face, spilling around her head in all different directions.

And then I turned, looking back at my mom as she poured my formula into the glasses.

My eyes widened.

"Stop!" I cried.

I sat up and straightened my back as I pulled the stool closer to the counter, then raising my hands and pleading with her.

"What is it?!"

"There's a *lump*!" I cried in panicked desperation. "Stop! I saw it!"

She reached out and picked up the glass, holding it up in front of her face, turning it and examining it. Every time, the same song and dance. It became a daily occurrence.

"I don't see any lumps. I shook it really well, Andrew. You watched me!"

I backed away from the counter, shaking my head. My face was shifted in panic, and my eyes were wide. I pointed. "I saw it! I saw it!"

My mother reached over to the drawer to her side and pulled out the small strainer with the tiny metal ears and the black handle, leaned forward, and picked up the offending glass. She looked at me, her face reassuring.

"I will strain it," she said gently.

My aunt sat down on the stool next to me.

Little did I know then she and I were destined to be pen pals and exchange letters back and forth several years into the future. She looked over at me. "Come on, Andrew. It can't be that bad."

"It *is*!" I put on the saddest puppy dog look on my face that I could muster.

"Can I taste it?"

I shrugged my shoulders as she took her finger and dipped it in the thick liquid in one of the small glasses. She brought it up to her mouth and tasted it.

"*Bleecch*!" Her face shifted in a grimace. "That's *horrible*! How do you drink this every day?!"

"I hate it," I said, and sat back in the stool, crossing my arms.

My mother turned off the sink water.

"Andrew, if I could pour it all down the drain and let you go to bed without drinking it, I would. But your body needs this. We go through this same song and dance, over and over. It is all of the vitamins and minerals you need to grow. You need it. Drink it."

In more recent years, companies have emerged that have been able to manufacture PKU nutritional formulas that taste good. As I am writing this, I am currently on three different formulas that are pre-made

241

in small boxes that can be sipped slowly because they are tasty. On the night I was sitting next to my aunt, her eyes widened with amazement as I slammed each small glass, one after the next, until all three were empty.

I felt like I was going to throw up.

I closed my eyes and held my throat, waiting for the feeling to pass.

It always did.

So yes, there was a rather unique way I would get my needed nutrition. I felt that I needed to make a connection with others, and so many people use food, and breaking bread together, as a means to connect. My feelings of isolation were present because I was unable, most of the time, to bond with others through food as my eating requirements were so foreign to most people, for many years.

And those feelings were bold faced and underlined when it came to mealtime.

When I was in first grade, I was in a small Catholic school, and although the teachers weren't nuns, the administration were. We all wore blue uniforms, and sat at our small, wooden desks. The school was usually strapped for funds, and in my early years there, there was no cafeteria to speak of. Lunches were brought into the classrooms, and students would eat right at their desks before heading outside for recess.

The cafeteria staff would bring in large aluminum containers that, in recent times, would be readily available at big-box stores, but during this time, in the early eighties, I don't believe those stores were as popular. When the big shiny box of hot dogs wrapped in white napkins was brought in through the heavy wooden classroom door, the first graders clapped and cheered, because lunch had arrived late that day.

I knew I couldn't eat that. But I still cheered with everyone.

I had my own PKU friendly lunch packed in my steel lunch box with my favorite cartoon characters on it, and that is what I would be eating. Not a hot dog, although I wanted to and wanted so desperately to fit in.

Shortly after the aluminum container of wrapped hot dogs had arrived, another cafeteria staff worker arrived with another aluminum container. It was of small milk and juice cartons, and I knew, in that container, there would be something for me.

One of those small juice cartons was mine.

I started cheering and clapping.

But no one else joined this time.

The teacher was at the front of the room, pulling the wrapped hot dogs out of the container and started handing them out to the students as the cafeteria worker carried the container of juice cartons to the front shelves, and placed them down next to the hot dogs. I quieted and noticed that my fellow classmates didn't share the same joy in a carton of juice.

I was in first grade during this time, and it's a memory I have.

Back then, I knew that the other students were cheering for something that I couldn't have. But I cheered with them anyway.

And when the cafeteria worker arrived with something I could have, I cheered again. No one joined in with cheering for something that I could have, but in those days, they didn't know. They just knew that Andrew arrived with a special lunch and didn't eat the cafeteria prepared lunches.

I simply wanted to fit in with the others. I was seven years old in those days, around the same time that my parents got divorced, and I didn't realize the gravity of that situation in my young life then either.

I had early memories, while carrying a small, powder blue blanket around the house, of watching them argue while standing at the kitchen sink. I remember my mother slamming the kitchen sink faucet down, shutting off the water, as she and my father raised their voices with each other, bickering back and forth.

I don't know what they were arguing about, and if I were to ask them now, they most likely wouldn't even remember. That memory was from a different house, several years prior to my experience in the first grade when no other students cheered for the juice cartons with me, but as I watched them argue, I thought that maybe my PKU placed a burden on the family.

I do believe that the only reason my parents got together was to have me, my brother, and my sister, and each of us has been extraordinary in our own right.

We are all unique, certainly, but for me, my difference was a matter of a life realized, or one wasted in a state of mental damnation.

There could be seizures, I would one day be told, or even severely limited brain development, and no hopes for a "normal" life; an education, a career, relationships, or any other aspect of living which humans held close could seem unattainable.

Unless I followed a restrictive diet, drank a foul-tasting medical "shake" every day, and regularly stab a lancet into my finger for bloodwork checks for the rest of my life.

When those words were first spoken, they weren't experienced directly by me.

I was in the blissful and loving existence of a newborn, and it was my parents who had heard the devastating news. There was a period of uncertainty, and a wonder of what this new, mysterious condition could be, which, they were told, afflicted their seemingly normal newborn little boy. It was two weeks after I entered the world, which is when the test is typically taken: a small prick on the heel, followed by a wail of crying; impressions of bright, red blood on paperwork to be sent to a lab for analysis, and then the news. Every newborn is tested.

You were tested.

But the condition is quite rare – it only affects, roughly, one in 20,000 individuals – and that one person just so happened to be me. Most babies are just fine, don't have to follow the diet, or have the same uncertainties which my parents did.

I was one of the first babies to be diagnosed at birth; one of the first babies to be placed on the restrictive diet, which, the doctors claimed, would allow me to experience a normal life.

They hoped.

Prior to the period when I was born, testing and dieting did not exist. There was no treatment then for PKU. And those who had it were sentenced to a life in which they failed to thrive and required assistance from birth to death. I consider myself lucky – not only to be born when the treatment for PKU was brought to the world (I was considered a "poster child" for PKU dietary management), but also lucky that both of my parents, and my siblings, had taken ownership of my well-being.

As a young boy, I didn't understand the concern in my parents' eyes as they would look over at me, as I would play, watching my friends run around with hot dogs in their hands at the barbeques as I would hold a bag of cut carrots and celery. I would fidget and bite my lip when they offered me some of their hot dog and I sheepishly said no. Even when they questioned why I didn't take their offer of shared food, I didn't understand why I had to say no in the first place. There came a point when it became routine, and somewhat commonplace, for me to reject offerings of food from friends, and friends' parents, as the way I ate was simply that: it was just how Andrew ate.

I remember nights at my father's house, later after my parents' divorce, when we would order pizza, and my siblings would make sure that I removed the toppings that I could not eat – which was basically all of them – with the exception of the vegetables.

"It's just bread and sauce," they would say to me. And it was. But even with the bread and sauce, I felt as if I was included, having somewhat the same items which everyone else had been having. And I had gotten used to it. It was just the way that I ate.

I had been given a daily allotment of protein equivalents which my body could tolerate without symptoms of phenylalanine toxicity, the substance which my body is unable to break down, in my blood. Despite everyone's efforts, not every day went perfectly, but most went well. I had learned to drink the foul tasting "shake" to get the vitamins and minerals which I would otherwise be missing in my nutrition.

And I always wished that I could sit down and eat a hot dog at the barbeques with family and friends at the lake, but for me, it would be a bag of carrots and celery.

I knew then, even as a child, that depended a lot on the success of the diet. My mother and father were dealing with myriad unknowns when I was an infant and toddler, but by the time I was nearing school age, the system had formed to manage my PKU.

And while the pizza may have just been bread and sauce, to the casual observer, who did not understand the nuances of the diet and how phenylalanine can build up in the bloodstream to toxic levels, that bread and sauce still had a significant amount of phenylalanine in them.

The PKU community calls it "phe" for short. It sounds like "fee". And I was allowed a certain amount of "phes" each day, and if I would exceed that threshold, then symptoms of elevated "blood phe level" could take over: irritability and mood swings, inability to concentrate, and skin conditions were the milder symptoms.

Still, despite the challenges, we continued as a family unit and from the casual observer's perspective, we probably seemed normal.

As the middle school years wore on, I didn't find it odd that I used to collect school supplies, including old desks, and used to "play school" in the basement. My little sister was my only student; I collected used textbooks when the schools were disposing of them, and I always treasured the out of date "teacher's editions", which would give me instructor's notes in the columns, all the answers in red, and a new confidence.

I was a teacher.

At my own fictitious school, of course.

In the basement, with my sister as my only student, but she was an attentive pupil. I believe she loved the afternoons with her brother – actually, I know she did. I remember when I assembled lesson plans, gave homework assignments, and had an entire classroom in one section of the large basement of my childhood home; I had managed to collect a good five or six old throwaway desks.

Over time, my school grew.

Some of our shared friends who lived on the same street would come to the house in the afternoons and play with me and my sister; I don't remember anyone, at that time, thinking that I was different. But then, young children are typically non-judgmental, and that was the time that we all chose to play school, typically right after we got home from real school.

I begged my mom for a chalkboard.

"I need it for my class!" I would tell her over dinners at night. During those years, I was in middle school, and my parents were already divorced. My mother was working, raising us as a single parent, and arriving back at the house after we all played school.

I was always the teacher. At the time, I was certain that I would become a teacher in my adulthood.

I had no idea that I would become an author whose books became available online throughout the world. Back in those days, I seemed to naturally gravitate to the role of being the teacher, and my sister, as well as some of the neighborhood children would come over to our house, and I would teach from old edition schoolbooks that I managed to get hold of, and we would all continue to learn, after the school day, until our parents all returned from their work days.

As I remember it, the chalkboard was an intimate bonding experience with my father.

In the years when my father and stepfamily lived nearby and I was spending the weekends with him, we built the chalkboard together, as well as my wood carved racing derby car for Cub Scouts which we made together, carved from a block of wood, for my derby racing contest.

The chalkboard, however, had a different purpose, and I remember days when we spent together, cutting and measuring the wood, and finding the right paint that transformed a large, flat board of wood into

251

a chalkboard that could be erased, wiped clean with a sponge, as a fresh slate. But it was the bond with my father that I got through several of those projects that have kept us close throughout our lives.

When I was a child in middle school, I started to have a sense that I was different. I wasn't involved in sports at that stage of my life, and that seemed to be the culture to connect with other boys my age. I had many memorable moments in my childhood with others at school, however most of my memories were of my interactions with the teachers and faculty. At that point in my life, there were many adults in my life who appeared to be looking out for my best interest.

And I gave them my trust in that.

Some of them were teachers who were educating me. Others were trying to ensure that I was embracing some social and physical activity, which, even though I dreaded at times, I needed. And I appreciate their efforts. Still, there were those adults who helped manage what I had always perceived as a shortcoming: my metabolic disorder, Phenylketonuria.

And despite my ability to pronounce the multi syllable word as a small boy, the word was always abbreviated by three easy to roll off the tongue letters.

PKU.

I never knew as a small boy what great efforts my family went through to ensure my brain developed normally. As I had experienced these differences throughout my life, it simply seemed normal to me. I was told that I was the "poster child" for PKU, although, at the time, I didn't know what it meant. I was told that I could not eat foods that had protein in them, because the phenylalanine was something which I had an allergy to, and would build up in my blood and become toxic to my nervous system.

What I did know is that I was different.

And the first thing that I noticed, even as a small child, was that I ate differently from all the other boys and girls.

Yet still, when looking back, I wasn't really all that different, was I? I didn't really think so, at least not when I was a child.

Sure, I was self-conscious when changing in front of the others for gym class, which extended into high school, and I never really understood why. Even now, many years later, I don't really understand why I seemed ashamed to have my shirt off in front of other boys. But weren't many of us a little self-conscious in the gym changing rooms while going to school? The other boys seemed perfectly comfortable.

But they were chatting about sports, and other things that I seemed to have no talent for or interest in. When I was a student in school and I was dreading physical education class, I knew that it was something I wasn't interested in. I was always picked last for any sports team.

I felt different and still do. Is there anything wrong with being different? Of course not. Now, it's celebrated. Then, I was not yet aware of that transition coming into my life.

When I sat in high school Geometry class, I used to stare off in the distance, watching the clock count the minutes, a hard rock concert playing in my head, and I remember chewing on my pen. I had the end in my mouth, chomping on it as the saliva washed through my mouth, listening to Guns N Roses play all of their hits at chest thumping volume. Of course, in my head. A private concert, just for me.

"Andrew?"

I looked up and over towards the center of the room.

The teacher was a tall and robust woman. Her short curly hair made her appear as if she was wearing a helmet, and she stood with her hands on her hips, looking over towards me, like The Terminator. I had my book and notebook spread open on my desk, and I looked down for a moment. What were we working on?

Of course, I had no idea.

I was listening to the concert in my head.

I put the pen down on my desk slowly, as a bright, clear pool of saliva dripped from the cap, now in a mess, filled with teeth marks. "I…" I said, slowly, nervously paging through the book.

"Can you go to the board and complete the steps to the proof?"

My heart started pounding in my chest and my face grew hot.

I could never grasp the concept of a geometry proof, and despite my cheating during the high school years, and despite my attention deficit due to the high levels of phenylalanine in my blood, I joked with the friends I had found that I flunked my mid-term exam for the class and squeaked by for the year with a passing grade of 60.

"That's a D, Andrew," my mother said as we reviewed my report card. I had argued that my mind wasn't meant for math. And she argued that I would have much less difficulties if I stopped cheating.

The cheating had to stop.

CHAPTER ELEVEN

For a guy who is different, I sure seemed normal, at least in my eyes. Throughout my childhood I worked to blend in and normalize myself, fearing being found out for being different. Until I finally reached the stepping stone on my journey where I was inspired to embrace it.

From a casual glance, I appear to be a pretty regular guy. At least, I believe so.

I suppose I could be the quintessential "guy next door". I stand five foot six inches tall, possibly five foot seven with shoes. Although when I was in my twenties, I had this misconception that I was five foot nine. I'm not really sure what led me to believe that nonsense, because I am much shorter than I thought I was at that stage of my life.

My weight also rarely fluctuates, usually I am about one hundred fifty pounds, give or take a few pounds, but I did gain some during the period that I thought it was fun to lift weights, and put on some muscle which I hadn't had previously.

That was a phase, indeed.

Another time, while living in the south, I gained some "chubbiness" all while discovering the joys and calories of southern cooking but then shed it after leaving the south.

All in all, I appear fairly average.

My hair is sandy brown, but it was true blonde when I was a small boy. Now, as I write this, it is lightening once again. Sun kissed, perhaps. Or possibly because of my Phenylketonuria.

Or simply getting older.

Over the years I have learned that PKU can cause fair skin and light hair. Although my hair darkened when I was a teenager, it lightened again when I moved south, closer to the equator and, therefore, closer to the sun, but despite those little nuances, I continued to consider myself pretty average.

I had no idea that I was destined to be extraordinary. Nothing ever occurred to me.

I found out, though, that there is an extraordinary part of my life which I had to gradually discover over the years.

It turns out that Phenylketonuria is extraordinary.

The metabolic disorder known by three letters, PKU, was one of the things in my life that made me special. Do I enjoy having PKU? Not really, to be honest. I wish I could eat what I wanted, when I wanted to eat it. But as I write this, as a middle-aged man, I know that eating whatever we want, whenever we want it, sure, we can do it. But there usually are consequences.

Those of us who have to remember our sodium intake may crave salt on our pasta or French fries or wish for that next fast-food indulgence. Can we do it? Can we shake the salt on our dinner plate and hit the drive thru lane again?

Of course, we can.

But our blood pressure very well may rise; the added sodium might interact with medications, and our lower legs might swell a bit the next day from water retention. Or our cholesterol levels may rise from the saturated fat in the Chalupas and Big-Macs.

It was that logic which revealed to me that the three letters that I have been living with my entire life really, perhaps, aren't that extraordinary at all.

Or were they?

When I was a little boy, I didn't know that I was destined to become a critically acclaimed author. I didn't know that I would become a hospitality management professional or spend my entire time on the Dean's List while attending a well-respected university in Philadelphia. All I knew, when I was a little boy, was that I wanted to fit in with all the rest of the little boys and girls.

I wanted to be one of them.

I would watch them play, laugh, and interact with each other. I always made an attempt to fit in, but I always felt a little…different.

I remember when I was in kindergarten, I stood in my overall jeans, the shiny buttons clasped together over a colorful striped long-sleeved shirt. I shoved my small hands shoved into my pockets. The teacher wanted to see my hands, but I kept them shoved in my pockets. I don't remember what she said, but I do remember my classmates gathering around in a circle, watching me watch the teacher, who bent down and looked at me, her eyes wide with concern.

"Andrew! Is there something wrong with your hands?"

I kept my hands as deep in my pockets as they could go and looked around the room at my classmates. They stared at me, their eyes wide and inquisitive, possibly wondering why I was having this interaction with the teacher.

But as she finally coaxed me into taking my hands out of my pockets.

I drew them out with an ashamed look on my face. I had the puppy-dog sad eyes, and my classmates moved in closer to see what the teacher was looking at. "Take your hands out, Andrew. Let me see."

I raised my palms and looked at them as the teacher gasped.

I looked down and saw what appeared to be large swaths of dead skin hanging off the palms of my hands. I wasn't concerned as some of my classmates leaned in and giggled.

"What happened to your hands?" the teacher asked.

A little girl pointed at me, teasing. "He put glue on them!"

I did, I knew it, and I felt my face grow hot.

Guilty as charged.

As some of the other little boys had done, I put a small lake of bright white glue on my palm and danced around excitedly as it dried. In all honesty, I'm not really sure why none of the other little boys had the same interaction with the teacher as I did, but I was the one who was singled out. As I learned over the years, I am special.

We are all special.

We are all unique.

And there is no one else in the entire vastness of interstellar space that is quite like each of us.

That is a quote that I hadn't been aware of when I was a little boy in kindergarten class, examining my small hands full of dried glue which was peeling off, resembling dead skin. I was destined to write that quote, decades later, and look back towards the past.

I would analyze the lessons I have learned over the years.

I remember my mother, when she would hold my hand, walking into church on Sundays, when I was still a small boy, and she would always remind me of the notion.

"Each of us are different," she would say. "All of the millions and billions of people in the world…and no two are exactly alike. Even twins are slightly different."

Those words inspired me to observe people, which eventually led to the quote.

The quote "You are special, you are unique, there is no one else in the entire vastness of interstellar space who is quite like you" had been birthed from the words of my mother. They were words which had rattled around in my childhood mind; I remembered hearing them. And back in those days, I knew what they meant. But I didn't have the same interpretation of them as I do now, nearly four decades later.

As a toddler, and throughout childhood, my mind had become a sponge.

My mother was steadfast in preserving my mind. She and my father had listened to the words of the doctors when I was a mere two weeks old. "Your child has PKU," they said. "He is part of the first generation of PKU babies when we have treatment. But you must follow it rigidly. There can be no deviation. Any increase in the phenylalanine blood levels can have a disastrous effect on the mind and the central nervous system."

"We need to breast feed him," she said.

The doctor's eyes widened as his mouth dropped open. "Absolutely not, Mrs. Mengel!"

My father placed his arm around my mother, as she looked down at me, sleeping soundly on her chest. "He needs the cerebrosides so his mind can develop properly," my father said, looking up at the doctor.

I believe the gravity of the situation was clearly understood. My parents were told not to take the path of introducing human milk into my body, for the protein would be devastating to me.

But it wasn't.

It was measured, and my mother and father knew me, like no other. And my blood levels were generally fine.

They were the sculptors of my mind. Over the years, it has proven to me, and to others, that someone with PKU can not only function as a normal person in society, but also can have the potential to be extraordinary.

In the days when my mother held my hand walking into church, telling me about how unique and special I was, she was raising me alone as a single parent, for it was in the days after when my mother and father had gotten a divorce.

But her words stayed with me.

And somewhere, in my mind, they rested, and waited, until I discovered my destiny as a writer. Was it in my destiny to become a writer? Was the reason why my journey was full of challenges in place to drag me through lessons? But I was destined to be a writer. Wasn't I?

Is that extraordinary?

But how can one *become* extraordinary?

Is it through good deeds, and a sense of purpose, and contribution to the world? There is certainly a sense of fulfillment for many who do good deeds. I have always believed that people are inherently good. Certainly, there are a few bad apples, but the bunch overall is wonderful, sweet, and delightful. One bad apple can spread to the bunch, but if the rotten fruit can be removed, the rest can flourish.

So, does doing good deeds make one extraordinary?

They certainly could.

Would one consider a philanthropic billionaire extraordinary if they created a foundation which changes the world for the better? I'd imagine that it would. That philanthropist would most likely be featured on various media sources and touted as one of the great leaders of the generation.

Or what if there is something extraordinary in each of us?

Different things which didn't require vast sums of money. Hidden talents or undiscovered life callings. Could someone who travels to an oil spill to wash the crude off wildlife in a desperate attempt to save their lives be considered extraordinary?

Or how about a single mother in a run-down inner-city apartment, working shifts at a diner while struggling to pay the light bill and keep the heat on. When she comes home, after a long shift, still in her uniform, she gives her tips to the sitter and starts making dinner for her hungry children who she hasn't seen all day.

Is she extraordinary?

While my mother was a single parent, she was not the diner waitress.

After she and my father divorced, she worked for a family friend who was starting a small business in their basement. She was able to keep the bills paid and keep the lights and the heat on for me and my two siblings while working each day. In those days, my sister and I were in middle school, and frequently walked to the local library together to wait for her, and along the way we would stop at the penny candy store.

The penny candy store had a small and easily overlooked façade on the corner of a large green Victorian style building in the charming downtown area in the small town that we all grew up in.

We were a lucky family, despite being a single parent family. When my sister and I went to the penny candy store, we each had a dollar, and were each able to get a fairly large bag of candy to enjoy (the candy was sold by the piece and was literally only a single penny per piece) and enjoy it in the cool library air conditioning while we waited for our mother to finish her shift at work and pick us up.

We were lucky because we lived in a safe and desirable community. Our father helped from a distance, and our mother always managed to keep the lights on, and the heat on, and our bellies full of food. On the weekends, she would find herself in the kitchen preparing special foods that were PKU friendly for me to eat. She wanted me to be able to eat as much as I wanted, not have to stop after a few bites because I might be receiving too much phenylalanine.

She would research low protein, and no protein, baking powders and flours, which were available, but costly.

She always managed to find the money for these costly items.

A box of low-protein pasta may cost ten or twelve dollars, but she managed to order it by the case, because she wanted to make sure that I had plenty of food to eat, and that I developed and matured just like any other boy. That my mind was protected, and my intellect developed properly, despite the constant threat of high blood levels of phenylalanine, which become toxic to my body once certain levels are experienced.

As such, that toxicity tears at my emotions, shattering my dopamine levels, and causing periods of overwhelming discouragement, and irritability.

Mostly, my mother didn't want me to be like the PKU babies who were born before me.

The doctors told her and my father that the consequences of too much blood phenylalanine were severely compromised brain development and neurological distress. And she wasn't about to have that.

When she and my father had finished speaking with the doctors after I had tested positive for Phenylketonuria, the questions mounted. Would Andrew have a normal childhood? Would he be able to attend the same schools as his siblings and friends? Or would he have to have assistance throughout his life?

And then came the word extraordinary.

There were times when everyone in my life, my mother, my father and my siblings, each had a part in what had comprised my childhood. But most importantly, the formation of my mind.

Although my mother was the captain of the ship, the other people in my life, while I was a child, had their own parts to play in not only the development of my mind, but also my development as a person. When I look back at the stepping stones that are behind me, I think of them as angels. And they really were.

And angels, always, are extraordinary.

PART THREE

THERE IS NO ONE ELSE QUITE LIKE YOU

CHAPTER TWELVE

I continue my gaze up towards the night sky.

In the years when I have been writing this story, I have become much more connected, not only to the Earth and the cosmos, but also to nature, wildlife, and spirituality. I have learned that when we view the stepping stones before us, they travel in different directions leading to separate outcomes for different people. It has taken me my entire life so far to become cognizant of other cultures and values, which I have learned to deeply respect and want to explore how others see the world.

After my father moved out of state, I approached my mother about spending the summers with him and my stepfamily. My mother was very supportive of this idea, and while there were concerns – not because anyone questioned any other family's capability of managing PKU – but because my mother was so heavily invested in the development of my mind, that the thought of anyone else taking care of those responsibilities appeared to induce anxiety. But my mother and father communicated and have always had a bond together through their children.

My father found doctors in his local area that could draw my blood while I was there.

It was drawn weekly and would be mailed in a tube express back to my home state for testing. And they purchased a bread machine and all of the ingredients needed so I could make my own bread while I spent the summers at their house, two states away.

It was summer and I was in high school.

While these were years of rebelling against the treatment and I cheated – mainly in the school cafeteria – during the summers, yet when I traveled to spend a full two months with my father, stepmother, and others two states away, I stopped cheating.

The summers when I traveled to see the new family, I stopped feeling the need to rebel against the diet. It became more of a normal thing, with my mother and father continuing to work together to manage my care, despite being divorced and separated by physical distance, something clicked in my mind.

I wanted to be successful.

And both sides of the family would help me do it. The college application period was approaching fast, and there was no way that I would be accepted into a decent school if I continued to eat the things that were damaging my mind, as I would not reach my potential.

My mother has always been a hero and an angel to me, but my father, I have always looked up to his success and wanted to be successful like him.

It has been argued by many over the years that a child benefits most from positive influences from both sides of the family, and those summers that I spent with my stepfamily, I believe, had a very positive effect on my development as a person.

The cheating naturally seemed to stop.

Looking back on those years, I don't think it was a decision I made consciously.

I seemed to lose interest in eating the foods that I could not have.

It was not all the summer trips to my dad's house, because my family back home was very encouraging when it came to music, and I joined the school marching band and concert orchestra.

Finally, I made some friends.

I had somewhere healthy and positive to channel my energy, rather than spending time focusing on food.

"I am choosing hospitality management as my major," I told my mother and stepfather while we stood in the kitchen, surrounding the giant peninsula countertop. I flipped the pages over and examined the personal information I had so carefully printed.

"You did such a nice job with my prayer meeting reception," my mom said. "Do you remember that, Andrew?"

I looked up from the paperwork. My mother held an oversized mug and was lifting her teabag out of the cup. "Yes mom," I said.

She beamed. "You did that, and you were only ten!"

My stepfather leaned on the counter and picked up one of the pages of my application and started to examine it. "This may really be a calling for you, Andy."

"Well," I said, as I crossed my arms. "I am not going to do anything with food. They have required courses that I have to do in the program, but once I get a job, I don't want it to be food related."

"That's understandable," he said.

That upcoming summer, I would be flying out, one last time, to visit my father and stepfamily two states away. As I would live with them for two months at a time, I had a room which I was able to stay in while I was there, and it felt like a second home to me.

They purchased a bread machine to make my mother's recipe, and one of the first things I did after my plane landed and my father and stepmother picked me up from the airport. I had two large bags that I hoisted over my shoulder. I was straining form the weight of my compact disc collection. Earlier that day, when walking through the airport on the east coast with my mother, I shifted the bags on my shoulders.

"I feel like I am a seasoned traveler," I said. "I've been doing this for several summers now."

My mother let out a chuckle. "If you were a seasoned traveler, that's all you'd have with you. Just those two bags."

"But I need all my clothes and things!"

She shook her head as she walked me to the gate. "What do you *have* in those bags, Andrew?"

"It's all my CDs! I can't be without them." She nodded as they started to call boarding my flight. "When you become a more seasoned traveler, you will learn that you don't need to bring all those things with you."

"Yes, mom, I know."

She reached her arms out. "Now give me a hug. I'm not going to see you for two whole months!"

We hugged and I turned slowly to join the boarding line. She watched, and I could see the look on her face that I would always come to know, whenever saying goodbye to my mother. She was happy and sad at the same time, and I could see it in her eyes.

I used to feel guilty leaving her and the others for two months in the summer.

I remember watching the weather channel while visiting my dad and his family, and I would always look for the weather back at home. I would see how hot they said it was getting, and I was wishing that they would experience some cooler weather.

We couldn't afford air conditioning in those days, and I would know how hot the house would get.

It used to cool down at night, and we would all sleep with big box style fans humming and blowing the cool air in from our windows.

I remember my mother going around the house in the mid-morning in the summer, closing all of the windows. "It's going to get hot everybody! Close the windows and close the shades!"

We all made every effort to keep the house as cool as possible, without the use of air conditioning.

As I exited the plane and walked through the terminal several states away, I shifted the heavy bags on my shoulders, straining under the weight, and raised my head.

My father and stepmother were standing ahead through the throngs of scurrying travelers, smiling and waving. By this time, my senior year in high school, they were used to my visits. They were excited to have me, and so were my step siblings.

When they lived close to us on the east coast before my father was transferred two states away, I had become close with all of them. During those years, I would go over to their townhouse, which was about ten minutes from my mother's house, and would spend the weekends with them. Sometimes, my brother and sister would come, but most times, it was just me.

The interstate summer trips were always me.

"Andrew," my dad said. "What's with the big bags?"

"Hi Andrew!" my stepmother said, as she reached over to hug me. "We're so glad to have you back!" She beamed as she looked at my bags.

"I have my CDs with me, so we can listen to them."

My dad and stepmother looked at each other and nodded.

As we all headed towards the escalator which led down towards the baggage claim, my father turned to me. "On the way home, we will stop at MCL Cafeteria."

My face livened. "Oh, I love them!"

"We know," my stepmother said.

"You can get the vegetable plate and everything," my dad said.

And I nodded and agreed, we retrieved my suitcase of clothes from the baggage claim, and all walked to the car.

There was something about going to see my other family where I also felt at home; I was welcomed and loved, just as much as I was back on the East coast with my mother, and my brother, and sister. Everyone enjoyed my visits, and when the end approached, I felt the same anxiety I did when leaving for the trip from my mother's house.

Everything was taken care of.

My father took me to doctor's office visits, two states away, to draw blood from my arm, which was new then, at least for PKU. I still did not look forward to the blood tests, but lying on an examination table in a doctor's office with a rubber tube tied around my upper arm and a small needle.

I still remember the sting of alcohol.

"It's a green top, heparinized tube," my father reminded the nurse who was drawing my blood. She nodded. "Yes, we have them, Mr. Mengel."

And then she looked over at me. "Are you ready?"

I climbed up onto the examination table, shifting myself to get comfortable. The paper crinkled beneath me as the sharp smell of alcohol hit me. I felt a chill on my arm as the nurse rubbed the small, cool wipe on my arm.

"Does it matter which vein I use?"

I shook my head. "Doesn't make a difference to me."

She tapped on my arm, while tightening the rubber tube around my upper arm.

"This one looks good." I looked up as she turned around, holding the needle up in front of her. "You ready?"

I nodded.

"There's going to be a tiny pinch, but it will be over in a few seconds."

I closed my eyes, felt the pinch. And waited.

"All done," she said cheerfully, as she placed a cotton ball on my arm. "Now put some pressure on there for a few minutes. You can hold your arm up too if the puncture starts to bleed."

I help up my arm for a few moments, while swinging my legs over and sitting up. After the nurse wrote my information on the small sticker on the side of my tube, she handed it to my father."

"I just need your signature here, indicating that we released this specimen to you," she said, handing him a pen. He signed his name and took my tube of blood.

"That was pretty simple," I said. "Painless. I've been starting this back home, but in the past, my mother used to have to jab my finger with a lancet. I dreaded blood tests. They were always the worst."

The nurse nodded. "Yes that does sound painful. That's great that your dad got you set up here for your visits. We can certainly draw your blood for you, so your dad can send it to the lab. I've heard of PKU. That testing is important, all the time, Andrew."

I nodded and my father and I left the exam room. "Yes, I know. I just wish that one day I could stop all this. If I could take a pill instead of drinking that awful formula and stop with these blood tests. No offense to you, of course."

She held up her arms. "None taken! But yes, we do need to find a cure for PKU, Andrew. It's an extraordinarily difficult diet to manage. One of the worst. But best of luck with it. I have confidence in you. I know you will do well."

CHAPTER THIRTEEN

As I write this, I am celebrating my 44th trip around the sun.

And as I am writing *this,* I am past my 46th trip. And now, I am on my 49th trip around the sun.

Fifty is looming.

When I look back at the writing of this book, which has essentially become one of the more significant purposes of my life, I take a pause.

I reflect quite often on why this book has been so challenging for me to write.

I've written numerous books, mostly fiction, as writing has come quite easily to me. I remember sitting in my high school creative writing class, writing stories in the years before I discovered that I had a passion for storytelling. In my college years, I continued the development of my literary mind, still unbeknownst to me. While my major was practical and businesslike, which I have learned is a must for any author or artist, my elective courses have proven to be a tremendous step for me.

I took Psychology, and Sociology, numerous language courses, as well as the study of fiction and film on the collegiate level. Still, I was unaware that I had the deep passion within that was yet to be awakened.

This book is vastly different from my fiction; however, I have employed my storytelling skills in crafting the journey to provide a sense of what it was like to be there. As this book is based on a true story, my story, I have taken a painstaking effort to ensure that the scenes — the memories — are as accurate as everyone remembers them. It's been quite time consuming.

Yet, in terms of the difficulty, that mostly came from looking deep within myself. This story is truly tearing off a bandage. I have procrastinated on this project more than any other.

This chapter is similar to my thirteenth book that went into publication in 2022, *Mona Lisa, Becoming a Ghost*. That was the one that won the award for best supernatural fiction. I call it my "Lucky 13", as it was an homage to one of my favorite stories, *Frankenstein.* It received the award for being a unique take on supernatural fiction, which, I was told, had not been seen before. Would I have been able to achieve something like this without the cerebrosides in the breast milk?

That part, I am unaware. There may be others with PKU as well, who have followed the treatment diet, and monitored their blood levels, and also went on to do something beyond the ordinary.

For me, I definitely consider myself lucky. To have people in my life who care about my mind and continue to do so.

I hear their voices in my head when I am tempted to stray off course on my journey, and I know they bring me accountability to my actions. I don't want to disappoint any one of them. Those in my past; those who have gone before me, and others who are in my life currently.

In the decades that passed after the days when I was a little boy, and I would stand with my friends and my bag of cut carrots and celery, the world has changed drastically. There were those who had a great deal of influence on my life, not only in my development as a child, but also had a hand in crafting who I am as a person today, who I must now visit in a cemetery.

But then, that is how life progresses, as it seems.

In the decades that followed my childhood, I proved to myself and others that PKU, when properly managed, need not limit one's potential. While I had some challenging years in high school, once I entered college, I found my first niche in life, and earned Dean's List grades, and graduated Cum Laude. After a successful career in Hospitality Management, I chose to step down and pursue my dream of becoming a published author, where I found my second niche and my creative passion. Had I been born just a handful of years before I had, my life might have turned out quite differently.

My mother and father divorced when I was seven years old.

I know that it wasn't because of the stresses that my special needs brought to the family; and I knew it back in my childhood as well. Coming from a broken home had nothing to do with my metabolic disorder, or my siblings, or anything else for that matter. It's just the way that things were. I quickly adapted to traveling between mom's and dad's – and felt equally protected in both places. Both of my parents understood my diet, at least to a degree, but it was my mother, who worked for years as a single parent, who deserves a great deal of credit for the development of my mind.

It was her mission in life.

She worked as a social worker for several decades and assisted just those individuals who her son might have become. After working long shifts for the state, she worked tirelessly in the kitchen, searching for foods that her son could eat without threatening his brain development.

My father felt fierce protection for his son, as he worked diligently to make sure there was always something to eat for me at restaurants, special events, and gatherings; particularly those that were centered around food. My subsequent writing became a way to express my appreciation to those in my life who helped me achieve what I have thus far, as it seems.

Once I became a published author, I was able to write books and dedicate them to those people in my life who all had a part to play in ensuring that I could be a functioning adult in society.

I remember those angels.

All of those people who have either helped me in the production of a book, or had a dedication page mention, have had a significant role in my development as a person. And that, in a nutshell, is the Three Letters journey.

It's looking out towards the sun against the distant horizon; it's seeing the stepping stones laid out before you.

And taking that first step.

Because the PKU journey cannot be made with one person alone.

There will be those who will be on the sidelines cheering you on. And there will be others who may not understand the condition; the creation of and fielding of questions will always be there. But that next step will also always be there.

And a point of growth.

Once your foot lands on that next stepping stone, there is a point of growth. It's something that took decades for me to learn. To realize that PKU was never going to hold me back from achieving my dreams.

It didn't matter what those three letters, those dark shadows which always followed me around, threatened to do. I did fight the darkness which seemed to follow me wherever I went.

But for most of my life, I did say no.

For much of my life I would believe that I am solar powered; yet events in my childhood may have offered me some insight as to why I held a fear of the darkness, and the unknown, and having claustrophobia.

It was those nights, while still a small boy, that were the scariest.

Those frightening nights may not have led to the novels which drew on my own fears of confinement; the books which addressed fears of premature burial and waking up inside one's own dark coffin might have originated from the horror films and books which I filled my mind with as a teenager and young adult.

But it was those nights, as a small boy, in the years prior to exploring the worlds of horror, when the terror squeezed, wrapping itself around me.

I woke up and gasped.

I couldn't breathe.

I didn't understand why I would wake up wheezing in the middle of the night, gasping for air; my wheezing in desperate struggling to breath as my lungs would close up, when my mother could come running, her hair mussed, her nightgown drifting behind her. She would pick me up in her arms as I continued gasping for air, and carry me into the bathroom. I would drape myself over the side of the tub, and other nights sit in her lap, resting my head on her chest, as the shower would fill the bathroom with steam, and my lungs would gradually open up, and I could breathe again.

When your life has been measured by three letters, there comes a point when one wants to throw away the ruler.

In the case of Phenylketonuria, which has been abbreviated in the medical communities as "PKU", the three letters always seem to follow me around, no matter how many times I've tried to shed them. Over the years I've realized that I've been an adult, and during the time when the internet had become increasingly popular, that the three letters which I'd been running from for as long as I can remember actually were some of the most poignant moments of self-discovery.

But let's start from the beginning.

This book isn't an homage to myself and the successes that I've found in life. Rather, the goal of this book is to help those who are affected by PKU. Whether it be a set of new parents, who receive the unsettling news that their newborn son or daughter has a mysterious condition; this book is for the PKU child, who may not understand why they have to eat special foods and why they must eat differently from the rest of their friends. This book is for the PKU teenager, who may find it a struggle to balance their bit of independence with a temptation for cheating on the diet.

This book is for the PKU young adult, who is now venturing out into the world on their own, in search of ways to make the diet work while balancing the early years of a demanding career. And this book is also for people like me, who have already experienced part of their own PKU journeys and desire to find new and innovative treatment.

Still, there is an overall goal of this book.

And that is to help people.

Anyone and everyone.

My story may not apply to your specific situation. But I know you, dear reader, have been through some shit. I know some of you may have had a past of things you have said or done that you have come to regret or wondered how things could have gone if you had acted differently. But we still love ourselves, no matter how unpolished we may be sometimes. Don't we? Still, you turned out alright, didn't you?

Or maybe you didn't.

Regardless, people do love you. Even if they don't have the emotional skills to show it.

Maybe you are reading this and thinking that crazy A.L. Mengel is making assumptions about someone he doesn't even know. And in that case, also, I am hoping that this book will help you as well. Nothing we did in my particular situation was done perfectly. And I did fall off track, as we all tend to do at times. I don't know what specific battle you are fighting, but I want to be here to assure you that battles can be won, even if they continue and are ongoing, they can still be won. We humans are an imperfect species, and there is nothing we can try to do that will change that fact.

So, I ask you, dear reader, to continue this journey with me. For it's perfectly imperfect, and so are we.

CHAPTER FOURTEEN

I don't want to come across as arrogant. I am not.

I'm very thankful for the angels in my life who have been there to guide me down my path, to help me make the right choices, and to help me back up when I fall.

I do want to let you, the reader, know that there is hope for a child with Phenylketonuria – and there is hope for all who carry a cross similar to mine.

I know everyone doesn't believe in angels.

But I do, and my mom does, and millions of other people do as well. And even if you do not, I know we all believe in humanity and purpose. Those aspects of life can drive us forward, towards breaking through our challenges, and seeing that, no matter what we may be carrying with us, we are not alone.

Our conditions that we have need not prevent us from following a dream.

With my journey, I now know that the regimented diets and supplementary formulas are, in fact, there for a specific purpose, and the PKU child *can* achieve excellence. If there are new PKU parents reading this book, that have myriad questions about the condition, I will provide information based on my own experiences and my parents who had a period of question and research after I was diagnosed as a newborn.

Two weeks into my life, I was crying, inconsolable.

My mother had been breast feeding me, but my parents did not know that the normal life sustaining milk that I was taking in was wreaking havoc in my tiny body. The two of them persevered, however. When I was placed on the PKU diet and my blood levels were under control, my parents agreed that I still needed to be breast fed.

When that avenue was presented to the doctors, they sternly warned them not to do it, for the breast milk had too much phenylalanine. The risk to my increased blood levels, central nervous system, and most importantly, my brain development was too great, they said.

"We cannot recommend it."

But they persevered.

My mother pumped her breast milk and froze it in containers. "It was so it could be measured," my father said, decades later, while I was having conversations, learning about what happened so this book could be presented accurately.

"She used to pump her breast milk, freeze it, and then would mix it with your PKU formula. We kept a strict diary, so we always knew how much protein you were taking in – and most importantly, phenylalanine."

"What becomes toxic to me, Dad. Yes."

On another phone conversation with my mother, she concurred that she used to measure out her breast milk. "When you were getting it, the doctors were so anxious. They had stressed so much that you needed to be on a strict diet. That you had to follow it without question, and that, they said, was the only way."

"But you guys gave me the breast milk anyway. You defied the doctors' recommendations."

"We knew that for your mind to develop properly," my mother said. "Was to give you the cerebrosides necessary for brain development."

"And so that is probably what made the difference."

For those who may be reading this book to discover my story of overcoming this obstacle, this book will also be my story of overcoming the odds, which in the case of PKU, especially in the time when I was diagnosed, the deck was stacked against me.

Yet still, there's something about people.

None of us are exactly the same. Although there are "identical" twins, no one is truly identical. If we were, how would others be able to tell us apart?

It's about both the achievements and the failures, and the journey I've been forced to take throughout my life, carrying my own heavy, wooden cross on my back, across stepping stones that reach outwards towards the horizon. I have learned that we all have different crosses to bear. The crosses vary in weight and composition. Some are lighter, made of wood, and others heavy as if made of stone. I have come to realize that my own personal cross varies in its own composition. There are days when everything seems easy. And others that I struggle getting through.

Still, I do not want to let three letters dictate who I am as a person.

The PKU journey has been brought with challenges, as most journeys are, mine has been relatively similar to others who struggle with medical challenges and metabolic disorders. For those with Diabetes have a similar path when they have to govern their intake of sugar, and test their blood regularly, all while monitoring their physical symptoms which have a tendency to masquerade as their disease. Be it skin issues, digestive issues, cognitive issues, and possibly more life-threatening ailments should a disease not be effectively treated. Or even if the disease is managed throughout life, sometimes the consequences of three letters reveal themselves, regardless of what type of letters an individual might subscribe to.

LL

There are memories which have cemented themselves in my mind from decades ago, and I remember every tiny detail as if the memory had occurred just the previous day.

I've been gifted with that type of mind.

I remember moments in pictures, as if I was an observer, watching a film of my past, and it has helped me as a writer. It permits me to remember what I was feeling on a particular day, how the weather was, how the room smelled. How I felt inside. What the people told me, how I was supported and nurtured throughout my life.

The day came, of course, when I would venture out into the world on my own.

The angels in my life were still there, but there were life lessons that I still needed to learn. I was on the cusp of adulthood, and it was time to cut the apron strings.

That morning, I remember so well.

I stood on the back screened-in porch, surrounded by a vast network of tall, shaded oak trees, as the warm summer breezes wafted towards me.

My mind was racing with uncertain thoughts; the anxiety which had its spiny fingers inside my body had tightened its grip. I knew this was something that I wanted to do. Others had told me that I had to have a college experience, outside of the home. On my own. But now…to flee the nest?

To live among the students in the dorm rooms, to wander the halls of the University without the need to get in a car and travel home each night, and to submerse myself into the college culture of intellectual studies, friends and fellowship. But with my PKU, and its clutches, it brought myriad questions: how would I be able to manage a strict, low-protein diet, along with the required medical monitoring, while living alone for the first time in my life?

How would I be able to get the required weekly blood tests to determine if I was managing the diet properly…or slowly and quietly destroying my mind and central nervous system?

I was elated when I was accepted during my senior year of high school.

My confidence had taken a beating when I scored far lower than I had hoped on the Scholastic Aptitude Test, and I thought, when I had gotten a three-digit score, that my PKU was a cross which had become so heavy that I would not be able to attend college, find a career, and live a relatively normal life. There were concerns that I would stray from the diet; peer pressure and temptation would take over, and I would undo all of the work that my mother, and the rest of my family, tirelessly dedicated themselves to while I was a young boy.

Their dedication was paramount.

If there hadn't been the level of commitment on their parts that there was, my life would have been a very different story.

I thought back to my childhood, remembering when I was first told that I was special, and then, the destiny of being different had started to form itself, although I remained entirely unaware. Not from that singular moment, but over time, as I would stand on the stepping stone and turn towards the past. I would see those moments. Each of them, which formed themselves together like a puzzle, gradually revealing a picture.

"You are special," my mother said to me, one day, while holding my hand as we walked into the massive Catholic church, a mere few miles from the house. It was evening; the sun had sunk beneath the horizon as the sky had awakened its fiery auburn beauty. It fought against the impending dark streaks of blue which reached across the sky from the east. I was a mere few years old, but walking, and I felt her large hand wrap around mine. Despite the chill in the air, the mittens I wore, and her gloves, I could still feel the warmth of her skin against mine.

I was her special little boy.

There was something unique about me, and it wasn't necessarily the different way that I ate. It also wasn't the medical formula that she shook up for me each day, while I would sit in the kitchen, on a small stool, leaning on my elbows on the counter, looking on, watching her as she scooped the sweet white powder from a blue and white can in a plastic shaker. She held it under the faucet and used her free hand to pull the handle as the water flowed into the powder, displacing it like the rapids in a river breaking up a snowbank.

She lowered the handle, and the flow of the water stopped.

"I'm going to shake it up to make sure there are no lumps," she said, looking down at me with a reassuring look on her face. She knew that I detested the medical drink and gave me that daily assurance that it would be lump free. Both she and I knew that I had to drink it daily, with every meal, day in and day out, for my entire life. I looked up at her as she smiled at me warmly, looking down at me, and I leaned back on the stool, and shook my head. "I don't wanna. Can't I skip it for today? Just today."

She slowly shook her head. "No, Andrew. I know it doesn't taste good. But your body needs this."

She gently placed the shaker on the counter, leaned down, and twisted the lid off.

She leaned it towards me as I hoisted myself up on the counter with my hands flat on the countertop, leaning forwards and peering into the shaker.

I examined the bubbles that hugged the perimeter of the shaker, noticing the colorful rainbow effect from the reflected light from above my mother.

"You see?" she asked. "There are no lumps. I shook it hard. You saw me. There aren't any."

I looked up at her.

There was a warm smile on her face, but I could see that she was tired. I knew, even as a little boy, that I was being difficult. But she knew. I may not have known then, as a little boy, that she would do everything in her power to make the formula palatable for me, because it was her calling at that point in her life.

I may not have known then, that, while watching her fish a glass out of the cabinet, and a strainer out of the drawer, she was doing those acts because she knew that my mind would demand it; if I hadn't drunk my medically prescribed formula, my body would not receive the nutrition it needed. It was quite a serendipitous activity.

My mind would suffer.

And she would not tolerate that.

It was those late nights in the kitchen, which played over and again, on repeat, through the years of my childhood. And, in my mind, I always feared the lump in the liquid. I hardly opened my mouth when downing the overly sweet, thick, foul-tasting fluid, for I remembered the one time that I actually had ingested a lump, I coughed dramatically with a sudden wave of nausea, waving my arms and grabbing my throat in a fashion that only I could.

But as we walked into the church that evening, my mother's prayer partners were standing in a circle at the front of the church, in the aisle, between the pews.

As my mother removed her coat and placed it on a pew, I promptly sat down in the middle of the circle, on the floor, raising my head, looking upwards at each of them.

Everyone stopped praying, and looked down at me, as I sat, Indian style, a slight smile across my face.

"He's going to do something special, Mrs. Mengel," one of the members said, after a few moments. "He has a given purpose; I can sense it."

Everyone was enthralled that I sat there, and then they continued their prayers. I sat, looking up, watching them watching me, as others agreed.

The destiny was about to begin.

Years later, as I was preparing to leave the house for the first time while heading to live on campus at my university, I stood in the front yard, under the shaded oak canopy of the forest of trees which surrounded my childhood home.

I was staring intently at the lime green minivan parked in the driveway.

The sliding side door was partially open, revealing a slew of boxes stacked inside. Most were open and I could see the colorful and messy contents inside. In my hands, I held a pair of white, rolled up sweat socks. I proceeded to the van and tucked the socks on the floor between a box and the floor mechanism of the front seat. I stood for a few moments and stared intently at the pair of rolled socks.

I could feel the tingling in the pit of my stomach. I didn't know if it was excitement or worry, but part of me knew, deep within, that it was nervousness. I hadn't lived away from my home, and my family, for my entire life, and while I was already in my third year at the university, I had reluctantly agreed that I needed the college experience. I lifted my hands off the socks and stepped back, turned and looked back at my childhood home.

It was a two-story colonial with white aluminum siding, nestled in a network of a tall, shaded oak canopy. The sunlight filtered through, as I took a breath and sighed.

A lot of memories resided there, many ghosts in those rafters.

As I stood on the side of the minivan, on the edge of the driveway, I turned and looked at the small tree growing in the center of the front lawn. I had planted it as a little boy. I looked up towards my bedroom window, where I had removed the screen and hung myself outwards, lighting a cigarette when I was a teenager and exploring smoking, as I had puffed and waved the smoke away in a desperate attempt to keep my bedroom from smelling like cigarette smoke.

The memories were there; they would always be there.

And while I knew that I was about to venture to campus to have an experience that deep down, within my soul, I knew I needed to have. I was going to make a new crop of memories; I knew that things would never be the same once that van door was closed. I reached my arms around my torso and hugged my chest, watching the house as it watched me.

I looked up again at the second-floor window to the right, towards my childhood room. It was the same room that I sat in, as a little boy, my arms spread out on the windowsill as I rested my chin on my crossed arms.

I had been waiting for my mother to return from her weekly prayer meeting at the church, and she was late. I had been in bed, and since my bed was next to the window, I opened it and felt the cool night air waft in. I could smell the damp night air, as I felt the gnaw of anxiety rise within the pit of my stomach. But in those days, I was merely a little boy. How anxious could a boy of that age be?

It turned out, quite a lot.

As I stood, years later, in the driveway, looking up at the same window that I looked out of one night as a little boy, in the grip of anxiety, which had become a side effect of my PKU, regardless of whether I was following the diet or not. In my early college days, I was starting to see how powerful my mind had become.

My mother always said that it had developed into a tool of brilliance.

I didn't realize I was an intelligent person until I reached college, once I got myself together and followed the diet, and achieved the Dean's List for each semester for the entire four years I was there.

Little did I know in those days that I was destined to become a critically acclaimed novelist.

When I stood on the edge of the driveway in front of the minivan, I turned back and looked at the socks. Simple white socks, folded neatly amidst boxes of just about everything I owned at the time. They seemed brilliant. As if they were brighter than everything else there.

I heard my mother approach my stepfather.

"You all set?" my stepfather asked. "This is a big step for you."

My mother gave me a hug, tighter than I could remember. I knew she was going to miss me. I was her little boy; I always would be. She and I had, and still have, a special bond.

It was her perseverance which truly preserved my mind from the ravages of PKU by ensuring that I followed the diet strictly; there was no deviation.

And for that, I am grateful.

It wasn't until later, after I had been dropped off on campus, after I had excitedly moved my items into my on-campus apartment, which my mother and I were able to procure through my need of having my own kitchen, that I learned how upset my mother was after they had dropped me off, and started on the fifty mile journey back to my childhood home.

"She was quite upset," my stepfather said. "The entire time we were driving home. This was a big moment. Not only for you, but for both of you. When you realize what she did – what she sacrificed to get you were you are – it was then that she realized that she was no longer in control of the situation. You have been her miracle for years, and you still are."

My time spent at college was short yet formative.

I followed my diet religiously; I used the small kitchen in my on-campus apartment as it was intended – to cook for myself and help maintain what my family had built – throughout my childhood, in an attempt to

308

thwart the ravages of Phenylketonuria on the mind and central nervous system.

Despite their efforts, I still had days when I would feel the effects of high blood phe levels.

I remember days when I would have a feeling of being overwhelmed by whatever situation my mind was attempting to process. I also remember PKU being a scapegoat for basic human emotion: there were days when my blood phe level was completely normal, and I still had a challenging day. Most of the time, however, the challenging days were caused by the cross which I had become accustomed to carrying.

My mind, however, developed beautifully.

It may have been the near perfect nutrition which the PKU diet had afforded me as a child; it may have also been the efforts of my family – and, in particular, my mother – in ensuring that I remained on an extraordinarily challenging diet while a little boy who wanted to experiment and discover the world – and its tastes too.

But my mind also had developed into something that was destined to betray me.

CHAPTER FIFTEEN

When I was still a little boy, as I knelt in my pajamas on my unmade bed, and looked out the window I was destined to look up towards, years into the future, when I would be leaving for college.

It was that night of terror.

Even as a boy, I knew sleep would not come to me until I saw the familiarity of the maroon Oldsmobile station wagon that we all called "the old red bomber" pulled up the driveway, and if I saw the familiar square headlights pulling up the curved driveway, winding through trees, the maroon body visible in the yellow hue of the lamp post.

If I saw that, my stomach would settle, and I would be able to lie down and let sleep gradually carry me away. That night, however, those familiar car lights didn't come, and in my impatient and anxious childhood mind, the minutes seemed like hours, and I started to imagine my mother in a horrendous car wreck. I could see her eyes closed as she was hoisted on a gurney into an ambulance, and I felt the spiny fingers of anxiety claw themselves into my body, as my stomach knotted, and my throat tightened.

The visions of horrific events have continued into my adult life. Over the years, I have learned to capitalize on the notion of my mind's propensity to head to the worst conclusion by writing supernatural thriller novels, but as a small boy, I was horrified.

Relief washed through me as I saw the car pull up towards the driveway.

I tossed the bed sheets to the side and tore out of my bed, and ran down the stairs, with tears streaming down my cheeks. My mother emerged from the side door of the kitchen, which led out into the garage. Her eyes widened as she looked down at me. "Andrew! What's wrong?!"

My muscles loosened as I saw her emerge from the back hallway, clutching her purse and jacket. The relief washed through me, and I ran over to her, tears streaming down my cheeks.

"I thought you had gotten into an accident," I said, wiping my hands on my cheeks, as she hung her jacket in the front hallway closet. *"I saw it in my mind and everything!"*

She titled her head. "I was only at church, Andrew. I was only gone for two hours. Why did you think that?"

I struggled to answer because I didn't know.

Just mere hours earlier, she had tucked me in bed, snapped the light switch off, the music of Psalty the songbook flooded the room, which helped me fall asleep on the nights when my mind wouldn't let me relax.

This was one of those nights, it seemed, and the songs that Psalty sang didn't seem to help.

I kicked the covers down the bed, relishing the cool air as it hit my sweaty legs. Mom should be home soon, I thought. And she would always know what to do when I couldn't sleep.

I propped up on my knees and cupped my hands around my face, looking out towards the front yard in darkness. I could see the dark spines of the trees against the dark blue night sky and then I looked down at our driveway.

The small dome of light cast a yellowish glow on the small stones.

She would be home soon, for certain.

She had to come.

A mere hour or two later, as I frantically hugged my mother tightly, my small arms reaching around her waist as she closed the front hallway closet door, she placed her hand on my back. "I am just fine, Andrew. Nothing has happened to me. I haven't died in a car accident. I am right here."

"I can't sleep, I can't, nothing is helping me," I pleaded. "I do everything. I listen to Psalty and the songs and *everything*, but I can't fall asleep!"

I sat down on the floor and cried.

She took me back up to my bedroom, as I saw the mussed covers on my bed and the window I stared out in desperation, and then she tucked me in bed for the second time that night.

Psalty's songs didn't have to play a second time.

For once my head hit the pillow, I could feel the grasp of sleep take over, my mind finally calmed. At last, mom was home, everyone was here, my brother and sister were still sleeping, everyone was safe, and I could finally relax.

$\mathscr{LL}$

And then my mind returned to the present.

Writing this book.

Digging deep within my mind, and having thoughtful conversations with those in my journey, remembering this story.

I remember taking a trip to my childhood home, a mere few years ago. I was already a middle-aged man, and the memories were fighting in my head to blast out onto paper.

During that visit, I was staring at the very same window that I had looked out of many years before, feeling the same gnaw in the pit of my stomach. There was a feeling that wrapped around me, but it was not a secure feeling.

I had returned to the home I grew up in, now as an adult. We were to celebrate my mother's birthday, and she and my stepfather had recently announced that they were planning on selling the house to downsize.

While I understood their reasons, I didn't want to accept them.

"A house is simply wood beams, and drywall, and nails," I told my mother on the phone the previous month. But I knew, when I spoke the words, that I didn't believe myself, and I know she saw right through it. "Our memories are with us," I continued "We take them with us." But I didn't want to listen to myself. For those memories had penetrated those walls and wooden beams. That house was not simply building materials.

That house had a soul.

I wondered if I truly believed what I had said to my mother. Is a house truly only nails and wood? I couldn't shake the feeling, in the pit of my stomach, that I couldn't fathom this house being gone.

Since I had already established a following for my writing then, I helped by filming a live video which was shared through their realtors as well as my online social media accounts. I helped, as they have always helped me, but I could not imagine a world where I wouldn't have this house to come home to. No matter how far I wandered, this home was always here.

As I gave my mother and stepfather a hug a few days later, with my destination to return to my Florida home, I wondered if I would ever see my childhood home again. I always enjoyed my visits, and I knew that the home was a tremendous responsibility for my aging parents, and that their downsizing was probably the most practical option.

Yet there was something inside me which longed for the past to return, that I wished the house would never sell.

I helped film as much of a professional video as I could at the time and shared it on my author page, helping my parents present their house for sale in a most appealing way. The video remains on my social media pages to this day. But in my heart, I hoped that I would not be successful. For when I was walking around the house in my video, the walls came alive. As I filmed, I remembered sitting on the stools in the kitchen, next to those same dark wooden cabinets, with my mother, sister, and brother, on busy work nights, when my mother would enlist the entire family to prepare dinner.

Years after my mother and father divorced and my mother returned to work and raised us, we would eat at the countertop which jutted out into the kitchen like a peninsula in lieu of eating at the table, because the table was reserved for weekends and special occasions. Me, my brother, and sister all would sit on the small, wooden stools which surrounded the peninsula.

But our mother chose to be different.

We had an old rickety highchair, which we all sat in as babies, which easily doubled as a stool with arms when it didn't have the small table which attached to the arms on small, steel runners.

But that was the chair mom wanted to sit in, and we all needed a place to rest our bones. It didn't matter how old or young we were, and it didn't need to be fancy. It just needed to do its job to support us after a long day in the world. Still, her children were always given the best seats in the house, regardless of what any of us thought.

It was those nights around the counter, when we ate simple meals prepared together, when we sat in the stools and mom sat in the old highchair.

We were all tired and stressed after long days of work and school, and we ate together and laughed, and sometimes argued, and shared our days with one another, that we became the family we were destined to become.

As I matured not only as a person, but also creatively, I started to understand how and why I was a special person. The night with my mother's prayer partners started to take form in my head over the years.

There's just something special about Andrew. Something different. He's destined to do something, Mrs. Mengel.

I was not called the offensive label as I was called in grade school, as I carried my silver boom box radio trying to fit in. So many days of desperation during which I was unaware of any rejection I received; nonetheless, I still pursued connections with people.

While the boom box may have been a catalyst of my attempts to fit in, over the years, the world slowly whispered into my mind, *you are meant to be different, Andrew. That is how the world will come to love you.*

I was not looked at with disdain like I was when in high school. Still, I found the arts. It was a shining beacon in a dark tunnel I seemed to be lost in during

319

my high school years. Music and entertaining called to me, and when I discovered my ability to tell a story, and be comfortable with people observing me, and them being entertained, I was able to truly embrace myself over the following years.

When I was approaching middle age and matured creatively, I took a leap of faith.

I left a nearly two-decade career in hospitality which I had selected as my college major, leaving the security of a regular paycheck and job, and I embraced my difference.

Still, I needed a job of some sort to pay the bills, and over the years of working in the hospitality business, I absorbed skills, which allowed me to be a bartender.

And in more recent years, I bartended.

The resort that hired me loved all my management experience in the hotel and restaurant businesses but didn't really understand why I wanted to step down and become a bartender. I told them I simply loved being with people and providing friendly and efficient service, and they hired me, without any specific bartending experience.

But I learned, absorbing all of the processes for mixology and creating cocktails.

When I was bartending, I was asked, along with another friendly and outgoing bartender, to work at a special event at the resort that had a 1980's theme. We were encouraged to dress in 1980's style clothing, and to keep it colorful, within the theme, and most of all…fun.

I thought of my various Halloween costumes when I was growing up a child, and the years when I was a television When I was around ten years old, my mother helped me make an interesting costume where we took a large moving box and hung it over my shoulder with suspenders and made a "screen" out of aluminum foil.

Also, when I thought of another Halloween when I dressed a drag costume as an "old grandma lady" shortly after appearing as the television.

I remembered when I carried my large plastic pumpkin around the neighborhood gathering candy. I swung my pumpkin, clicking along in a pair of my mother's high heels on the pavement, chatting boisterously with my sister and her best friend in our neighborhood.

I smiled at the memory.

I tried to think of something appropriate to wear for a major resort pool bar near Disney World.

And then I thought of my vampire costume, which I won the school costume contest for being "scary".

I simply reminded myself to stay in character, no matter what happened or what people said.

And it won me the award.

The bartending job gave me a way to keep the bills paid while pursuing my passion, and on the afternoon before the special event at the resort, I stood in front of the mirror, wearing my 1980's-style costume.

I looked at my face, remembering those days as a child fondly, but this was different.

I was an adult; I had responsibilities, and I was about to put on a costume and head out in public. And it was nowhere near Halloween.

I looked down.

My jeans were too-tight and rolled at the ankles; I wore bright fluorescent socks and too-many gummy bracelets on my wrists. I held the bright green wig in my hands.

"Do you have the courage to do this?"

My voice was small against the silence of my bathroom, as I held the wig, a bright, fluorescent green headpiece with long locks wisping out in every direction.

"Are they going to make fun of you? Are you going to look ridiculous?"

It would be the first time I would appear in public in an outfit which I felt most effectively expressed my personality. I looked at myself in the mirror, holding the wig against my chest.

It covered the oversized pink MTV logo on my t-shirt.

"You are special," I told myself, echoing my mother.

The words were echoing others in my life who saw that I was unique, well before I did. Yet when I stood in front of the mirror, preparing myself to appear at an event themed around the decade of my childhood, I recalled the story my mother told me, about the night at her church, when I sat in the middle of the circle of praying and talking adults, as a small boy, sitting in the middle of the floor, looking up at them. My mother remembered vividly. "They knew you were going to be special," she said.

I put on the wig, and it immediately started to itch.

The price of entertainment, I thought. *The price of bringing joy to others.*

I stared at myself.

My bright green hair was spilling out in all directions around my head, a perfect complement to my bright t-shirt, fluorescent fingerless gloves, and jelly jewelry.

It felt like I'd headed back decades, to a time when my angels were protecting me under their wings, when I was still discovering the world, and enjoying life – a PKU life – as much as any child could.

I looked like I stepped right out of the 1980's. I could still feel a twinge of uncertainty building within, wondering if the resort would like the costume. But the child-like confidence that I felt won.

And I walked out of the door, heading out in full costume, to drive to the resort, and appear publicly for the first time to entertain others.

You're going to go a long way, kid.

PART FOUR

WHO AM I?

"You are special. You are unique. There is no one else in the entire vastness of the interstellar space who is quite like you."

- THE EUROPA
EFFECT

CHAPTER SIXTEEN

One of the questions that I believe we all share is likely the first of a series of questions we ask ourselves. It's a question that likely enters our minds, perhaps without our awareness, while we are still infants.

Who am I?

As we are new babies, just entered the world, after our parents take care of us and our most basic needs of survival – food, water, shelter, and love – as we reach a point when we begin to *explore* one of the first things we may wonder enters our minds on the first day, when we encounter a mirror.

The mirror never lies, and it shows us who we are. The baby will stare at a mirror in wonder, seeing themselves for the first time. People in middle age might have bathroom discussions with themselves, as I have on numerous occasions. I believe that these periods of self-reflection can help us better understand who we truly *are,* beyond what we may choose to share with the world.

It's like a celebrity.

Image is upkept when they are in the public eye, but are they the same person when at home, behind closed doors? Quite possibly not. No one can be "on" at every moment; I have found that there need to be periods of relaxation and reflection, to be the person who they *really* are.

As I am writing this book, I have found that I still suffer from some of the same problems, the same issues that I did when I was a younger adult.

Now as a middle-aged man swiftly approaching fifty, I am dealing with different issues that I did while in my twenties. I take daily medication to help regulate my blood pressure; I witness the new and gradual, and sometimes sudden, changes in my body and my appearance as I prepare to start the next era of my life.

In 2019, I produced a series of videos, which I placed on both my Facebook and YouTube channels, called #TheEraOf. It was an examination of how art learns from life. A lot can happen while a work of art is created; life always continues. In the series of videos, I examined my own journey, where I originated from, and how what I had experienced in life may have affected my art and writing. The series was composed as a journey, each set with its own hashtag title.

The second chapter, known as #Rejuvenation, is the video where I revealed my PKU to whomever viewed the series.

Telling the world about my PKU, after I became a published author, was a hurdle to overcome which had been longtime in the making. At that point, I had already conceived *Three Letters*; in fact, I conceived the title and wrote some of the book around 2009 or 2010, but at that point in my life, I was still only dreaming about writing books.

I knew that, from the writing I did in my college years and as a young adult, that I had the desire to become an author. I looked up to the authors whose work I read while growing up and was inspired to write. Years followed, and I found my niche in the hotel business, primarily in banquets, catering, and eventually, the alcoholic beverage business within the hospitality industry.

After I had taken the tremendous leap of faith and moved to Miami – alone and knowing not a single soul in the city – I had people move in and out of my life, some of whom were distractions to my eventual journey to become an author; others who have remained in my life for decades and have proven to be angels.

Miami, though, was an interesting step in the journey.

After my belongings had been carefully packed and loaded with a moving van line which I researched and hired myself, I asked a friend from Delaware if he wanted to make the trip down to Miami with me as I didn't want to make the trip alone. After I had said my goodbyes to my mother and my stepfather, I got in the car and started to pull away.

I turned out of the driveway onto the side street, and saw them standing together, side by side, watching me. And waving.

This was the start of my new journey.

I spent my last night in New Jersey with my parents, because my belongings had already been shipped with the moving company. My college buddy was already focusing on other things and other people, and I knew I needed to spend some extra time with my mother.

It was an exciting yet terrifying time.

The night before, we sat around the dining room table, as I opened cards and gifts for an early birthday present.

"This is going to be the first birthday that you won't be around, Andrew," my mom said. "You're going to be a big twenty-five!"

"I know, I know," I said, nodding and laughing and reading the cards. I looked up at the others. It was a small, intimate gathering around the table. My mother had baked me a birthday cake, although my birthday was still a month away. But by then, I would be living in Miami, over a thousand miles away. My mom was there, along with my step father, and my mom's best friend, also a social worker, who had bonded with her after working together for many years and going to the same church.

I focused on my mom's best friend as I held up her card. She smiled and nodded enthusiastically. "Yes! Open it!"

I slid my thumb under the flap and drew the card out, and some cash fell out onto the table.

"I know you're going to need money with this new adventure," she said. "I know it's not much, but I thought it would help. Put some gas in the car for your drive. Buy a beer when you get there. Whatever you want."

I beamed. "Thanks so much!" I rose from my chair and gave her a hug.

But when I was slowly pulling away the next morning, as I turned back to look at my childhood home one last time, I saw the look on my mother's face.

It was the look of a mother saying goodbye to her child.

I had seen a version of the look on her face when I moved away to college, but this time, it was for real.

She smiled, but there was a look in her eyes that told the story. Her child was leaving. I imagine her mind was racing with questions. How will Andrew manage his PKU so far from home? Will he be able to get his bloodwork done? Will he have his formula? Would he eat the right food?

I had never seen so much sadness fight its way through a smile and a wave.

I felt the emotion build inside me as I drove away and they were no longer in sight. I felt the tears well up in my eyes, and I wiped my face with my free arm. The sadness was quickly replaced with excitement, uncertainty, and a list of things to do. I had to get to Delaware to pick up my friend who had agreed to drive down with me, I had to get to Florida to have a few days to settle in before I started the new job which I was moving down for in the first place, and then there was so much uncertainty.

I was leaving the nest.

For real this time.

This was something I knew I would be able to accomplish despite carrying the three letters of PKU, because I always had a vision of my future while growing up. I was young, hopeful, and optimistic.

I had yet to have life slap me in the face, I was always under the watchful protection of my family, but now the wings had parted, and I was released to fly on my own.

I could look out, see and experience the world, and it was waiting for me. I was allowed to fly out of the nest, for the very first time, and go out and experience a life that would only be painted on the canvas of my destiny.

I could soar over the mountains, towards my destiny, flying above as I would guide myself from one stepping stone to the next.

As the miles from home added up, my friend said something profound to me, which I still remember to this day. "I'm going down there for a few days," he said. "But you are going home. Doesn't that feel weird?"

It sure did.

The feeling hadn't pierced me yet.

I was headed home.

I was driving and navigating the heavy south Florida traffic on Interstate 95, as we were swiftly approaching Miami.

I sighed. "I suppose I never thought of it that way," I said. I looked over for a brief moment and saw him tilt his head to the side and smile warmly. "Is it starting to hit ya?"

I bit my lower lip.

I was really doing this. One way or another.

Everything I owned in my life was in boxes, in some random moving truck, hopefully making its way down to Florida. But I didn't really know. The anxiety I felt was always there; it remained in the background, and I could easily shove it into a box so long as I could leave it there.

I was so happy that my friend chose to make the trip with me, and I cherished the bonding we experienced during the journey south – I was beaming at the first Miami sign on Interstate 95 just south of Arlington, Virginia. I remember stopping in Savannah, crashing at a motel; ordering pizza and watching movies together, and finally…his taking me home to the new life I was preparing to start.

When we approached downtown, the glittering skyscrapers rose from a crowded, busy cityscape like soaring pastels on an expansive artistic canvas. I chose the vibrant, colorful, sprawling metropolis of Miami to transform into the butterfly I was destined to be.

CHAPTER SEVENTEEN

During the first days that I was in Miami, I drove around with my friend, getting a lay for the land, and a feel for the people.

My personal belongings had not arrived yet, and we spent a lot of time over on Miami Beach, particularly South Beach, because we were young; we liked to have fun, and I loved going to the beach. After some lazy beach days, we crashed on the floor in my new, empty apartment, which soared above the city.

On the last night before he was supposed to catch a flight back to Philadelphia, we decided to go to dinner together.

After my college years and working for a few years in the hotel and restaurant business, I had become savvy with menu ordering for my PKU and felt more confident to special order something for a dietary need.

It was the early 2000's, and in those days, restaurants were just starting to embrace people with special dietary needs, and the menus were no longer ironclad.

I started to enjoy going out to restaurants after working in restaurants.

I gained the confidence needed to look at a menu – which at first glance – would have nothing on it that someone with PKU, let alone a number of other metabolic disorders, could have.

A very different experience from when I was a child.

On that night, the last night with my friend, when I looked at the menu while sipping on my cocktail, I gasped.

My friend looked up from his menu. "What is it, Andy?"

I set my drink down and let out a chuckle. "I can't believe this," I said. I flipped the menu around and pointed. "It's a Portobello Marsala! I was reading through the ingredients. I can have this!"

He leaned forward as I showed him my menu.

He looked at his own menu, flipped it around, and nodded. "That actually looks pretty good. With mashed potatoes and broccolini."

I was the happiest I had been at a restaurant for as long as I could remember. In the coming decades, restaurant special ordering became far more common, and the day came when there would be menu items which I could have, and in some cases, I would have a *choice*, and that made dining out a much more pleasurable experience.

But after dinner, we went to bed for the last time, took some additional blankets, and some other items I had placed in the trunk inside. I handed one of the blankets to my friend. "Well, after today, it's just you, my friend."

I nodded. "I know. It's so weird. The last few days felt like a vacation. Thank you for coming down."

As we settled on the floor on opposite sides of the empty room, as it was getting late, and dark, and the sleep was starting to take over, he spoke again.

"It's going to be all you, starting tomorrow."

My eyes opened, and I lay awake on the floor, staring above. The room was dark, save the auburn hue of the evening light spilling through the window on the ceiling.

I nodded off for a few minutes, and then awoke, as I could feel the twinge in my stomach.

I watched the ceiling fan spin above me, as my mind started to race.

This was it, and he was right. As of tomorrow, I will be alone. In a strange city, all by myself. I knew no one. I had no friends. All I had was a job to report to in two short days.

But nothing else.

There were cases of my formula in boxes on the counter that I had brought down with me, but that was all I had. My mother had saved a few emergency cases of formula in her garage for me in case I needed it, but now, everything fell on me.

And that was it.

The next morning, after I dropped my friend off at the airport, I drove back to my new home. I was navigating the Dolphin expressway downtown, where my twelfth-floor high-rise apartment was, near Biscayne Bay, and as I pulled my car into the parking space in the garage, I nodded as some passersby politely but knew no one.

I thought about turning back the clock as I pressed the elevator button, and when I reached floor twelve, I walked down the silent hallway towards my door.

1202.

My new home.

I turned the key and pushed open the door.

There it was. My own personal space.

I was the boss of me, and I was in charge of my life. Open rugs, a sliding glass door which opened to a small balcony which I loved when I first arrived days prior with my friend, because it had a breathtaking view of the downtown Miami skyline.

But now, things are different.

Silent.

Now, it was just an empty apartment. And I was all alone. And I cast my thoughts to the past.

L

Ah, to be seventeen again.

Would any of us want to turn back the clock?

I think if you ask ten different people, you might get a wide variety of answers. Possibly even ten. And if someone were to ask me, would I want to journey back in time?

When the passage of time can be like a series of stepping stones reaching out towards the horizon, I consider each stone and the aspects it has brought, or what the new stones may contribute to a new destiny.

When I envisioned the image, as I stood on the stepping stone, I glanced ahead at the other stones, as they seemed distant. When I turn my head, and look at where I came from, I see how much I have grown. Not only as someone with PKU, but as a person.

The stones seemed closer together.

More in focus. But would I want to return to the past? Redo things, eliminate my mistakes?

Writing this book has directed my thoughts towards the past, as I would stand on the stepping stones. I would turn back to where I came from, and I would be able to see all of the decisions I made.

The things I did that were *right*.

And what I did wrong.

Even if I knew it was wrong.

This book has given me a chance to come to terms with some of the mistakes I have made. I was never a perfect individual; and I would never attempt to portray myself as such. I didn't always make the right choices. And I didn't always do the right things. I know I hurt people, and I wish I hadn't.

But we must always remember to learn from our words, our decisions, and our actions, and find it in our hearts to forgive ourselves.

I know there were times when I broke my mother's heart.

And other times when I broke my own, particularly when I lied about cheating on the PKU diet, or about my phase of smoking.

Still, I remember all the little nuances that make someone a unique individual.

I was born at 3:46 in the afternoon.

My mother would always be sure that I remembered. When I look back on my life, I sometimes wonder if those who are born later in the day are night people, and those who were born early in the morning were the early risers.

That spiritual, quiet, and purposeful time.

I was always fascinated by the night, and by darkness.

As a teenager, I devoured horror movies and novels as if they were to be banned the following day. I remember sitting in bed in those hot summer nights, with the fan roaring in the window, blowing in the cooler evening air, with a Stephen King paperback open across my knees, raised up in front of me.

I remember reading my favorite book, *Pet Semetary*, and I could envision the characters in my mind: Louis and Rachel Creed, arguing in the kitchen, and Louis spills a bag of flour.

"Oh, fuck," he said.

The scenes played out in my mind like a movie. I remember reading, and re-reading, the sequences when Louis and his friend Jud Crandall head through the woods to the Micmac burial grounds.

Terrifying, and captivating, at the same time.

Although I read that story countless times in bed late at night, scaring myself to sleep, I did what I learned was a faux pas from book aficionados: I folded down the upper corner of a page to mark my spot in the book.

There was the inspiration I found to write.

It seemed perfectly normal to me in those days, when I was a teenager, and, although I knew that my older brother respected books to the point that he hardly opened them up to read them, I continued the marking of pages by my folding ways. My brother wanted to keep his books in mint-condition. I would watch him reading in bed, and it was a very different experience than how I did. He would lay, hardly holding the pages apart to protect the spine, and peer inside to read the text.

Still, he absorbed the entirety.

It was somewhat different for me. For books that inspired me, somehow, or those that I felt like I needed to fully and completely absorb, I would read on repeat, over and over, until they started to fall apart. As if I needed that repetition to cement things in my mind.

And that is what I did with Stephen King's novel.

It's interesting how that book may have proven inspiring for some of my own work, as much of my own writing examines death and the mysteries of the afterlife, and frequently with a cemetery related atmosphere.

These speculating books I wrote, which have received positive critical reception, all came from the mind that was once that of a young teenager, who cheated on his PKU diet relentlessly during the high school years, who struggled with the reading comprehension section (and the math section, for that matter) of the Scholastic Aptitude Test (SAT), but still had a fascination with storytelling.

In the days after I took the SAT test, I groaned when I looked at the results, holding the paperwork in front of me, as I sat on the small, wooden stool next to the kitchen counter, while my mother prepared dinner.

I closed my eyes, sighed, and shook my head. "No school is going to let me in with a score of 927."

I slapped the paperwork on the counter and shook my head. I folded my arms.

"Andrew," my mom said. "Stop scowling. It's fine. You will find a school. But you need to get your diet under control. And you need to stop cheating. Your level is up."

I shook my head and scoffed, looking at her as she leaned on the counter, folding her arms. I steamed in the stool, leaning against the back, scowling. "I wish everyone would stop blaming PKU for basic human emotion," I said, thinking of my family telling me that I was irritable.

Like every teenager, those moments struck me.

But it was not basic human emotions every time.

Naturally, sometimes it was.

But when the phenylalanine levels increase, judgement suffers. As does mood. I have learned, over the years, that my most discouraged of days, my blood level is a prime suspect.

I am aware that these days, there are many things which make living with Phenylketonuria much easier than it was in the past. There are special foods which mimic the foods that a child with PKU cannot eat – such as hot dogs, chicken tenders, and similar items – which are strict forbidden foods in their normal form. But now, with the advancements that have been made in the treatment of PKU, children of today do not have the same inquiries from friends about eating special foods, and weird foods.

These special, low-protein foods allow PKU children to seemingly eat the same foods as their friends, even if the foods were simply imitations of the real thing. A PKU child is unable to eat the vegan "burgers" and "sausages" as those typically have a high protein content.

Now, PKU children are allowed to eat the same foods, modified for the PKU diet. The hot dogs look like hot dogs; the chicken tenders look like chicken tenders, and the hamburgers look like hamburgers.

But they are imposters, nonetheless. Formulated for the PKU child, to be safe to consume and blend in with the other children. They help quell the fear of being different, and unwanted inquisitiveness is lessened.

My mother always told me that I was unique, that everyone is. That we are all special, and throughout the entire world, there isn't another person in the world that exists who is exactly like each of us.

And there is an element of truth in that notion, I believe.

Consider identical twins.

To the casual observer, it might be challenging to identify who is who, and in that respect, the twins can be mixed up at times. Yet when one looks at the details, and considers each twin's own personality, there can be elements of difference, leading up to the point of total uniqueness.

One can argue that twins have an in-depth connection and understanding of each other that most do not experience. I am not a twin, and so I do not speak from experience, I'm afraid. But I am an astute observer, and I know several sets of twins, and I can see the similarities, and understand how people can incorrectly identify them. But I also note the differences which each set of twins exhibits.

Physically, they are similar, yet not exactly the same, particularly if they stand next to one another and the small appearance details, and personality traits, are considered.

And therein lies the notion that we are all unique in one form or another.

L

When I was a teenager, I hoisted my bedroom window open.

Mom was right, of course she was, she always was. But, in those days, the curiosity took over.

When I opened the window, she was at work, and I was determined to smoke. I felt like it was meant for me to do, and something, perhaps, I had done before. Perhaps in a previous life?

There was something fascinating about smoking, and as a child, I always admired people who smoked; especially older people, and women in my family, who seemed elegant and sophisticated to me. They would light their long, skinny white cigarettes, and I wanted to be just like *them*.

I didn't even inhale, at least not until I got to college. But I felt classy with a long cigarette, blissfully unaware that the work my family was so tirelessly doing to preserve my mind was potentially being for naught while I damaged my heart and lungs.

The next day, I looked for the two packs of cigarettes that I had swiped from the smoke hole, as I liked to call it. My mother asked me casually as she was preparing dinner as I stood on the counter, writing notes for my media production class.

"Andrew, I found something illegal in your room."

I looked up from my notebook. "What are you talking about?"

"There were two packs of cigarettes in your room, Andrew. Everyone knows that you have to be eighteen to smoke, and you aren't eighteen yet. So that is illegal." I took a step back, my hands raised in front of me, my head shaking back and forth rapidly. "Oh, those aren't mine!" I said. "A friend gave them to me to hold."

That was the story I concocted on the fly. Now that I am writing this, I know my mother knew I was lying to her. But still, she chose to play along.

"That's fine," she said. "But we can't have illegal substances in this house." She fished a pair of scissors out of the drawer and held them up in front of me. I looked down at the shiny blades as the overhead light gleamed on the metal. "Since they're not yours, you should go ahead and cut them up."

And that is what I did, right in front of her.

I took those two packs of cigarettes, and picked them up, six or seven at a time, held them in my hands with my thumb touching my index finger to form a circle, and snipped them up, and let them fall into the trash.

Despite this, my fascination with smoking continued, and there was nothing that my mother or anyone else in the family, for that matter, would be able to do to keep me from exploring it.

When I was in college, I was over eighteen, and I could buy packs of cigarettes in any convenience store.

I didn't have to sneak to a cigarette machine in restaurant vestibules to grab pack of cigarettes when I was a teenager. I had become known as a smoker around campus, and I finally learned how to inhale. I thought it was so cool when my classmates and I would stand outside, smoking together, telling stories, speaking as the smoke billowed out of our mouths, and connected and bonded together.

I was included, and I loved it.

Who am I?

More recently, as a middle-aged adult and while writing this book, I would rise in the early morning, before the sun came up. I would take the dogs out for an early morning walk, and the best time was just before sunrise, due to the intense heat and humidity in Florida.

I looked up and stared at the same night sky above me, that I had as a boy, with the same stars, and the same feeling of wonder. I gazed upwards in the darkness, as I listened to the leaves rustle around me, as a cooling breeze passed through. They had said we would see the planets if we got out of bed soon enough, before the sun, in the shroud of darkness, so we could see them.

In one view across the star scape, we could see them all – Venus, Mars, Jupiter, and Saturn. And if we were as precise as the astronomy aficionados, we might even be able to see Mercury as well.

There was something about it.

A feeling of awe which washed through me, as I stared up at the early morning sky, wiping the sleep from my eyes. My head had not yet shaken off the fuzziness, but I knew how small I was – how small each of us are – in the grand scale of the universe.

I had a hard time grasping the fact that I was looking at planets that I would never set foot on, but with the advent of modern technology and science, we have been able to explore much farther than we ever have during the course of my lifetime.

VOYAGER 1 was launched when I was a mere year old, and to this day, it continues in its journey. Yet when I would stare at the planets on this interstellar beach we call Earth, gazing at the dark and the stars, standing in the cosmic ocean, leading to a intergalactic journey through infinity, I wondered about myself.

My purpose.

The reason why I am here.

Why was I meant to take this journey?

To carry this heavy cross?

The carbon and the stardust showered on our planet, creating life; creating us, as we live, and grow, and thrive, and shine and exist and love, and hate, and question, and wonder, and dream, and create, and procreate…all in this biosphere.

Author Carl Sagan captured the sense of who we are as a species, and a planet, and a purpose, in his book *The Pale Blue Dot*.

But whenever I look up at the sky, I wonder about my purpose. And the questions that would flood my mind continued, as if they demanded an answer.

Who am I and why am I here?

In fact, what was the purpose behind this planet being the one planet in our galaxy that harbors life? How can our purpose be to simply exist on a single planet? Could we be meant to expand our knowledge of the vast universe in which we reside?

There must be life somewhere, still beyond our reach.

But mostly, in those days, when I was gazing up towards the sky, not only when I had been writing this book and taking the introspective journey, my wondering continued. It started many years before I had been writing this.

The journey simply gained more depth.

My mind has continued to learn, and experience, and process, just as all our minds do.

And it makes me think sometimes about my mother. And her determination to breast feed me, against the advice of the doctors.

As I write this, PKU has gained much more clarity into what it is, and how it can be treated, and how the mind can be preserved. And, also, how human breast milk can be incorporated into the treatment.

The human mind is a wonderful thing; something to be celebrated. To be developed and nourished.

It allows us to experience, and feel, and wonder, and dream, and love, and is the source of anything and everything about us from our birth until our death. To lose this ability sounds terrifying, and that is why the urgency was so prevalent when I was a child, in the years before we understood. And why, not only is PKU something that we now fully realize that must be taken seriously, for life, but also is a reason why humanity is desperately searching for a cure for Alzheimer's disease.

The mind is most of what matters to us.

Without the mind, our sense of purpose, of self-worth, of love, of dreaming, of familiarity with our family and friends, all vanishes.

So, I frequently ask myself, who, then, am I?

That's one of the questions I've been asking myself lately. When I look in the mirror, I see myself, sure, but I notice the coming of age.

Sometimes, I can still see the child within. Especially if I page through old photo albums.

I am still there.

But more often than not, I see the middle-aged man staring back at me. I now keep my hair cut short, regularly with clippers, and I miss the days when I had long, wavy hair which my mother had always said she loved when I was a teenager. We are all growing older, yet, somehow, still we remain youthful at heart. And our minds keep us with the same wonder we had as a small child.

When I was still young and living in New Jersey, in the years when I was an adult, yet still felt like a child, in my college years, I started to feel like I wanted to discover something more.

Something different.

There was an entire world out there, begging to be explored. In college, I respected my diet. I ate properly and got my bloodwork done regularly. I became determined and driven, long transformed from the hoagie and chicken leg eating procrastinating unfocused teenager. I knew that I wanted something more, something different.

There came the time when I felt the need to fly away from the nest, from the protection of my mother, and my family, and truly discover myself.

Who I was.

I remember, shortly before I moved out of state, driving home from campus in a snowstorm. It took me several hours to get home on the snow-covered interstates. While that was not the deciding moment, I knew, in those days, that I craved a warmer climate. I thought a lot about my Aunt, Uncle, and cousins out in California, and knew that, at their house, it was always beach-friendly weather.

I gazed out through the windshield, as the cars backed up behind each other in front of me. The red hue of the brake lights filtered through the falling snow, as the windshield wipers whooshed the flakes away. I could see the dark layer of clouds above; the seemingly misty air as the snow fell, and the slushy darkness reaching under the tires.

Stay in the dark paths, I thought. *Then the car won't fishtail in the crap.*

I saw the cars and the snow, but the images were replaced with blue skies, and sunshine, and swaying palm trees. I have always loved the area where I grew up, and to this day it always feels like I am coming home when I visit, but in those days, I longed to experience something different.

My PKU was starting to fall into the background.

In those college years, my blood levels were running perfectly, and my confidence seemed higher than it had been, at least concerning the Phenylketonuria.

Could I do it?

Could I move somewhere far away?

As I finally pulled the car into the snow-covered streets of my neighborhood, I saw the beauty of the snow covering the trees; the heavy, wet white flakes piled on the trees, weighing down the limbs, creating a wintry canopy like in a C.S. Lewis novel.

I eased the car on my street as the limbs reached downwards under the weight of the snow, and I noticed that my street looked like a completely different street when the trees were bending under the weight of the snow.

I looked at the world, my own ecosphere that had always been my haven of protection. I noticed how beautiful everything looked when the trees bent downwards covered with snow; they were the same trees that I had always known yet now appeared undeniably unique.

Perhaps being different was perfectly okay.

Was it time for me to grow?

Throughout the course of my adulthood, I have come to understand that there are countless people who are marginalized simply for being different from what, at one time, may have been considered the norm. Is normalcy truly a destiny?

As society grows and progresses through time, so did I. At the start of my adulthood, I initially did not stray far from the protection of the nest.

During the first year after I graduated college, I live in a small apartment adjacent to my stepfather's house, as he had moved to live with my mother and create a home together after they had married. His mother lived in the house, who was approaching eighty, and I was able to experience some freedoms from living away from home without the assistance of living at college.

It was a baby step on my journey towards a full and real adulthood, and I moved some furniture from the house I grew up in twenty minutes east to the rancher and the small apartment.

The apartment was tiny, but it was my first place. I felt like I had left home, but I was still kind of home.

I remember calling my mother. "Mom, the power is out!"

I stood in the tiny kitchen, about the size of a large closet. It was a little square, with a small stove, refrigerator, and a few counter tops and cabinets. It was fairly basic but met all of my needs.

I was now bathed in darkness, but I wasn't calling my mother in a panic because I needed to make my dinner and there was no power.

I was calling her in a panic because I had discovered the wonders of the internet – still in its infancy in those days – and I wanted to chat with my newfound distant friends in the chat rooms on America Online.

My mother seemed amused. "Andrew, that happens. The power goes out sometimes."

I shook my head, pacing around the tiny kitchen. "I know! But I can't understand this! I am sitting here in the dark!"

"Andrew, this is part of being an adult. The power goes out from time to time. It will come back on eventually."

There was a soft knock on the door which led from the small apartment up a small set of stairs to the main house. It was my grandmother, holding some flashlights and candles. "Here you are, Andy," she said, holding them out to me. "Now be careful with the candles. We don't want to burn the place down. We already had one fire here. Don't need another one."

I took them as she disappeared from the door and back into her laundry room and long, galley style kitchen which was attached to the door of my tiny apartment. There was always family nearby, more than a phone call away, mere steps away.

Regardless, I only stayed in that small, attached apartment for a few months, as I wanted to move closer to my job, the city, and shopping. Still, the power did come back on, and I prepared my dinner, and sat at the computer, rejoicing in connecting once again with my new online friends.

When I wasn't in AOL chatrooms, and immediately after graduating college, I was hired at the same local hotel where I had worked my co-op job while in school studying my Hospitality management program.

I had been a supervisor in – all places – the full-service three meal restaurant. Despite my declaration when I was younger, I was intently stating that I did not want to have anything to do with food due to my PKU, foodservice was what embraced me with open arms.

Upon graduation, I was hired as an Assistant Banquet Manager, for a large hotel not far from the Philadelphia area, and I was successful there for several years. I became the acting department head after the actual department head suffered an injury and was no longer able to work. My PKU was there, I was managing it properly. I was drinking my formula; I was not cheating on the diet.

I was a leader for a staff of up to 100 servers, bartenders, housepersons, and set up staff while at the tender age of twenty-two.

Things were going smoothly but I did desire something more.

I enjoyed what I was doing, but there was something deep within me that knew I was meant to do something else. I've been told before, and there may be an element of truth to it.

I remember being told this. "You know, Andrew. A few people may remember Andrew the Banquet Manager. A few more will probably remember Andrew the Bartender. But how you are truly going to be remembered – what will shape your legacy – and how you will truly be remembered is as A.L. Mengel *the author.*"

Yet, in those days, I maintained my course of growing in the hospitality business.

As the days passed at the hotel and the busy banquet weekends piled up, one evening, when I trudged back to my small apartment attached to the house, I sat at the computer and did a search.

I wanted to see where I might be able to go. I loved my family, but part of me knew that it was time to grow.

Everything was going so well, with my job, my PKU, and my life. But something felt like it was missing.

When I called my buddy from college, in the chef's office, I removed my jacket, folded it in half and placed it on the desk. My college friend had scoffed and taunted about a topic discussing gay and lesbian people. And when speaking with him, I remembered our family friend from that frigid New Year's Eve, back when I was still a small boy.

"You know," I said. "Boys really do kiss boys. And girls really do kiss girls. And everything, really, is going to be okay, regardless of that."

The line was quiet as I knew he was pondering what I had just said. I listened to the ambient kitchen noise which wafted into the tiny office. I heard the clanking of pots and pans, as cooks called out for the next plate up. I gazed out of the glass window, watching the cooks place brilliant green and orange vegetables into large, aluminum, rectangular hotel pans.

"You still there?"

He scoffed. "Of course, I am fine with all that, Andy! I am progressive. I think all that is fine."

"It's important that two people who are living together share the same values. So, I will fly to Cleveland," I said. "I can get a ticket tonight, but it's going to be one way. You have the rental all lined up?"

"Yes, yes, Andy. It's all done. Good *Christ* you're a nag!"

"Come on, bitch! I only have a few days for this crap. If we're moving all your shit out here, I only have a short amount of time. I can't take that much time off. This isn't a vacation!"

And a few weeks later, I flew to the Midwest on a one-way ticket, to help my college buddy move right back to the East coast, to be my roommate. I moved out of the small, attached apartment at my Grandmother's house and signed a lease with my college friend, on the top floor of a mid-rise apartment building, on the eighth floor, overlooking a shopping mall.

Now, it truly felt like I was living alone, away from the family, for the first time, even though my mother, and stepfather, and the house I grew up in, was a mere fifteen minutes away. My PKU clinic, which I visited regularly, was fifteen minutes in the opposite direction.

Close, yet far, at the same time.

Still, I always had a fascination with places outside of where I grew up.

I grew up in small-town Southern New Jersey, went to school in Philadelphia, and after college was the time when I lived with my college buddy as roommates in a high-rise apartment not far from Cherry Hill.

This was close to my job that I started shortly after graduation, and a few more miles down the road, was the PKU Program at Cooper Hospital in Camden, New Jersey.

When I was in college, I managed to move beyond the phase of food exploration, which had a profound and positive benefit in my life, and the summer trips to my dad's seemed to have helped.

Long gone were the days of chewing on pen caps and having a rock concert playing in my head while in geometry class; I was following the PKU diet. I was focused, and I was interested in the subjects that I was exploring.

In the past, in the year when I was applying to college, I sat at one of the stools at the kitchen counter of my childhood home.

"I want to own a casino," I said, not looking up, to my stepfather, who stood nearby in the kitchen, while I was completing my application for Widener University.

"Captain Hook's, that's right!" he beamed.

I looked up.

He was smiling broadly, holding a can of beer, and approaching the counter. He set the can down on the counter and leaned over the paperwork. "Is that what you're going to put on your essay?"

I looked back down at the paperwork and bit my lip, shifting my thoughts back towards my old notebooks. I loved to draw casinos, and I had an uncanny obsession with both Atlantic City and Las Vegas, partially due to my aunt and uncle. I thought of the letters that I traded with my aunt when I was a young boy, and perhaps, that inspired me. My aunt and uncle lived in Southern California and remained Vegas regulars at the time. Living on opposite coasts, we were separated by distance yet remained connected through words and wonder.

"I figured Hospitality Management would be a good major," I said, paging through the University manual. "A good way to gain the knowledge of the hotel business, right?"

My mother looked up from the vegetables she was chopping for a crudité.

"Oh, Andrew, that is right up your alley. Do you remember when the people from my prayer meeting came over?"

I smiled a half-smile as I examined the entrance questions on the application.

Of course, I remembered.

As my mother started to tell the story once again of when the ladies from church sat in our living room every Tuesday night, I would fill in my memories of the evening.

"Yes, and I remember, mom," I said. "I was in the kitchen, and I could hear you guys praying, but I started rummaging through the drawers in the fridge and thought it would be nice to put together a reception for you and your friends."

She smiled, shaking her head, eternally amused by the scenario. "What ten-year-old does that?"

"I did."

My stepfather leaned in closer, paging through my application. "That's why you need to do this," he said. "You have a talent."

"I didn't even know we had that wine," my mother said, seemingly amused at the memory, and returning her attention to her vegetable chopping.

As I continued filling out the application, I listened as my mother and stepfather talked further about the night that I catered a wine and cheese reception for my mother's church friends at ten years old.

I had heard it all before.

My mother had never ceased to be amazed that a young boy would be able to assemble a reception for multiple people, let alone with wine, cheese trays, vegetable trays, crackers and multiple selections of wine.

"It comes naturally to me," I told my mom.

I had fished the nicest wine glasses my family owned out of the hutch cabinet in the dining room, and I washed and polished them, setting them in neat rows at the end of the dining room table.

I could hear the prayers and discussion in the living room, which was opposite the dining room. I looked across the foyer as I was polishing forks and placing them in neat rows on the table, moving as quietly as I could. I saw the light filtering in from the living room, but the couches were not visible. I listened. About ten people? Maybe eight?

Years later, when I was sitting at the kitchen counter, filling out my college application, I thought back to the night when I was ten years old. After the prayer meeting had adjourned, my mother and her guests were ecstatic, and all enjoyed the fruit, vegetables, cheese, bread and wine.

I didn't know who I was when I was filling out that application.

At that time, I was who others had told me I was. The people in my life who helped me discover my own talents. When I was a young boy, I didn't know that I was talented enough to display a professional looking reception setup on my mother's dining room table at a moment's notice. It was others who had told me that I had that talent.

Yet in the subsequent years of my life, it took others once again to help me discover my identity, and to continue to protect my fragile PKU mind, even when they had no idea they were doing so.

Several decades later, when I was approaching middle age, I stood and looked in the mirror. The years of experience had drawn their lines beneath my eyes; I could see it as the light hit my face a certain way.

But as I stood in the bathroom of the tiny, shared apartment I rented, I had been examining the minute lines beneath my eyes. I didn't remember them being there before, but I had been getting over one of the worst colds of my life, which set in immediately after I finished my first novel. Maybe the haggard look was due to the illness?

During those days, I was living in Florida and was established, at least as much as one can be while still in their twenties. I was working at a hotel in banquets and catering. Still, I dreamed of being an author, and had finally finished my first novel. The bug had finally bitten me, and with the encouragement of my best friend, who sat with me and read through chapters, as my first beta reader, he encouraged me to write, and to keep writing.

And I finished my first novel, *Ashes*.

When I was a young adult, no one seemed to care about the PKU I had, because I kept it as a skeleton in my closet. I didn't tell anyone; I knew, at that stage of my life, how to manage the condition I knew of, and was constantly aware of it. When people asked why I was eating the way I was, I would respond, "Oh, I'm a vegetarian."

In those days, I used the trendiness of alternative eating to my advantage.

It was just after the turn of the century; the world, and especially the United States of America, was still reeling from the attack on the World Trade Center and the Pentagon. In this period, I had recently left home, drove all the way down the east coast of the United States, as far as I could go while remaining on the continental United States, and found myself in an apartment in Miami.

I had built my life in New Jersey, even convinced my college buddy to leave the Midwest and share an apartment with me not far from Philadelphia, and nearly walking distance to my new job, as a banquet manager at a recently opened Wyndham hotel.

When I lived with my college buddy, I was in my early twenties, scarcely out of college, filled with confidence, but feeling like I was running on empty with practical knowledge of the world.

"I want to move to Florida," I said, as my college buddy and I were sitting next to each other on the small couch I had been given from my grandmother's apartment, in our small living room in our eighth-floor apartment.

"What?!"

His head snapped around towards me, as the commercials started. "Miami?! You have got to be fucking kidding me!"

"Wait, wait," I said. "I want you to come down with me. You don't want to live in Florida?"

He scoffed, leaned back onto the sofa, and shook his head. "I'm not coming with you dude," he said. "You just moved me here! I don't want to move again so soon. And to Florida?! *What the fuck*?!"

I got up from the couch and made my way to the kitchen. "I will finish out the lease with you. I'm not going to leave you high and dry. Honestly, I want you to come down there with me. Don't really wanna go there alone."

"Then don't go?"

I heard him scoff again as I fished through the cabinets and pulled out the familiar blue and white can down on the counter and started scooping the white powder into the blender as my college buddy appeared in the doorway. "Drinking your white shit again?"

I nodded. "Yup." I knew he couldn't see me as he was sitting on the could and was watching TV. There was no way for him to see me.

But it didn't matter. I had made my decision.

He could come with me, or not. He was my closest friend from college, and maybe it was time to part ways. We had spent a lot of time together, but there was something within me calling me to head south. It was time to experience new territory.

The PKU formula that I had been drinking throughout my life had been degraded to "white shit", and I was perfectly fine with it.

It was shit, honestly. He was absolutely right. But the formula allowed my mind to normalize, and strengthen, and to have the correct levels of dopamine and serotonin.

And the formula was all I had.

I never grew into the taste, even though I had been drinking it for two decades at that point in my life. I scooped my six scoops of white powder into the blender and filled it with water. I was living in my apartment, seemingly on my own, with my friend from college living with me, with me wanting to leave the nest, and everything I had ever known, to flee from the angels which had protected me, and move across the country to Florida.

Anything could happen.

As I looked over at my buddy, I could feel the guilt coming on.

He was right; I had just helped him pack up his life and move several states away because I didn't want to live alone. And as I watched him watching TV, I thought to myself. Why was I doing this?

Why was I leaving the comfort and protection of my life, for the unknown?

Not much after, as I walked across the marble floor in the lobby of the Wyndham hotel, I looked at the small, printed page of weather for cities across the country. It was before the era of smartphones and carrying tiny personal computers around; it was the days when hotels would print pages out from a computer, and place them in clear, plastic stands on the front desk so people who were checking out could see the weather for the country at a glance.

As I approached the front desk with the heels of my formal shoes clapping against the marble floor, I scanned the page quickly and looked at the Front Desk Manager. She was on the phone, her long, curly blonde hair concealing the sides of her face. She looked up and smiled as she hoisted the long, coiled black cord away from her hair. She was one of my happy hour friends from the last hotel that I worked for, and we both were some of the staff that was lured to this new property. She smiled and beamed, still holding the phone to her ear.

I leaned over the front desk and whispered. "I think I am going to move to Florida!"

Her face shifted, her eyes widened, and she tilted her head to the side, watching me as I waited for her while she finished her call. After she thanked the guest and he left, she pulled me to the side of the desk and whispered to me in a hushed tone. "What do you mean, move to Florida?!" She groaned. "It's a little sudden, don't you think?"

I leaned on the front desk grabbed the small display of the printed weather across the country. I pointed it and shifted it around so she could see. "Did

376

you see the weather in Fort Lauderdale? Look! It was 89 degrees today!"

She nodded and smiled. "Yes, Andy. And it's February. I print those out every day and place them on the desk for the guests. I see the weather. So, you want to go down there for the warm weather? That's your reason?" She let out an amusing laugh.

I gestured my arm out towards the doors as they swooshed open. The chilly blast pounded into the lobby as the winds raged through, and the potted palms that were inside blew in the assault of the chilling wind, as fronds flew and danced. "You see that!? Another damn snowstorm. I can't take this anymore. I've been here for almost twenty years."

As the phone rang, she nodded, and lowered her eyes, looking down below the confines of the raised marble desk. As she picked up the black receiver and held it up to her ear, she mouthed *Touche,* immediately playing with the twirling black cord, wrapping it around her fingers. "Thank you for calling the Wyndham hotel. This is Cheryl. How may I direct your call?"

Like the theory I argued that PKU was a common scapegoat for basic human emotions, the weather was the scapegoat for the logic of picking up, suddenly, as it seemed. It was the other people in my life who viewed moving to Florida, well over a thousand miles away, may have been a rash decision.

I didn't hear them. Possibly didn't listen.

The weather may have been part of it, but in many of the unspoken reasons for my moving and essentially abandoning my life, and my protection I always had, was not something I was able to figure out until decades later.

And when I stood in that small apartment which overlooked the downtown Miami skyline, after I had dropped my friend off at the airport, I looked down at the two blankets on opposite sides of the empty room. The carpet was a standard rental beige, and there I was.

Alone, with no one.

But I was the one who made the choice to cut the umbilical cord. I was the one who decided to place the distance between myself and my family, my friends, and my angels. I didn't know then, and at that young age, that I needed them, but they were always there.

Waiting.

Patiently, for me to discover about myself, whatever it was I needed to.

When the deed had been done, I slumped down and sat cross-legged in my empty apartment.

There I was, in Miami.

Alone.

In an empty apartment.

And that is all I felt I had.

I hung my head, feeling the anxiety creep into me.

I closed my eyes and wondered when my things would arrive. If they would ever arrive. If I would be heading back to the car and driving back up the coast, with my tail between my legs.

Miami was no longer a vacation.

It didn't feel like home. My friend who came down to help me was now gone; my college buddy was still living up north; I was starting a new job in an area of a city that was big, busy, stressful, and crowded. Filled with people, all who were strangers to me. I could never remember feeling so alone.

What had I done?

PART FIVE

WHY AM I HERE?

CHAPTER EIGHTEEN

There are countless people who are not afforded the gift of growing old.

I remember, when I was younger, still a boy, thinking that thirty seemed so *old* to me. My parents had me at thirty. So, of course, that was old age. Wasn't it? When I now look back to when I turned thirty, I thought, then, that I had become a master of life. I had experienced so much.

Hadn't I?

Yet, that may simply be the cycle of life.

When we stand on the path of stepping stones, we look back with much wisdom. No matter which stone we stand upon. When I was thirty, I stood on that stone which crafted and guided that era of my life, during that time. My footing felt a bit firmer. The stone wasn't as slippery as the ones behind me were.

The waves had calmed, at least somewhat. The water was not crashing against them, at least, not as much. Or maybe I was more adept at maintaining my footing. And my balance. The thoughts which washed through my mind were now much different than they had been as my PKU continued to remain in the background, yet it was always there. At that point, I felt I had gained the wisdom I longed for when I was a child.

But the crosses remain, as they do for us all.

I have talked with many people during the writing of this book. I have learned that there are many conditions far beyond what I am facing, and in many cases, some of the crosses that people bear throughout life are far heavier than my own. Yet I feel that is part of what makes us all human. Our blood all runs red; our ears all hear the same sounds; our eyes all see the same things; our digestive systems are all *meant to work the same way.*

The food we eat is supposed to be there to provide us with energy and sustenance. But why do we have these conditions? Why can, what is meant to be a source of survival, food, harm us?

It's the mind which makes us unique, I've always thought. Not every food is good for every human, my mother always used to say to me. That wisdom, which has governed my life, and countless others with many different conditions which prevent consumption of the very thing that allows us to survive another day, week, or year, is what builds our connection.

Our minds, and our thoughts, can be manipulated by those who raise us, those who surround us, and those who govern us. But what truly makes us who we are seems to be located within the mind, somewhere, somehow.

Deep within. Therein lies our purpose. I had found it a difficult prospect to absorb, but isn't everything that we cannot fully understand?

It's all in there somewhere.

Years after my thirtieth year, when I was bartending, in 2017, I remember the eclipse areas of the world experienced. I had to work that day, and the resort I worked at was supposed to be in an area where the day would be dim but not fully darken.

Everyone had purchased those funny little cardboard glasses so they could look up at the sky, and the resort handed them out to guests as a complimentary token. Even though I was stuck behind a pool bar, I remember looking outside when the eclipse was happening.

When I raised my head from looking at the cocktail I was mixing, I saw that the daylight seemed filtered grey.

In the area I was in, it was not a total eclipse. For about ten minutes or so, it was like someone had taken a shroud and draped it over the Earth.

It wasn't dark; it was dim. Like the lightbulb needed changing.

We were in the era of smartphones, and I looked over at the guest. "Go," she said. "See it. My drink can wait."

I ran out from behind the bar.

I flicked the camera on and started to record video while making my best attempt to not stare directly at the sun.

Some of the guests looked up, wearing their funny glasses, and pointed at the eclipse, their voices quivering. "Oh, God, *that is so beautiful!*"

I could feel the emotion building within me.

I could let the tears flow, but I was working, and I chose to keep it in and drink in the beauty of the eclipse. Maybe I should have let it all out. For at that moment, we humans failed to point out our differences.

Business stopped, and no one would have cared if someone cried, and many did.

It truly was beautiful.

It brought us all together, as humans. Birthed from carbon and stardust which showered on our planet after the formation of the universe.

It was a reminder of that great cosmic ocean that we are floating around in, experiencing every moment, from when we open our eyes, until we close them for the last time, on this planet we all call home.

We humans have stared at the sky, whether during the day or under the veil of darkness, for millennia.

It's part of what we do.

I know every human being who is reading this shares the same exact questions I have, at least to a degree, because we all innately need a sense of purpose. Who hasn't looked up to the night sky, and gazed at the stars, even the planets at times, and asked the question *why am I here?*

Many forage paths of faith, science, and philosophy which can lead to a discovery of purpose. Still, the ultimate question remains. Why are we here?

Does anyone know?

Will any of us while we are still living?

Or maybe that is an unanswerable question? Or is it something that we may one day discover either through an explosion of inspiration or a slow and gradual reveal?

There are those of us who spend countless hours counting and watching numbers.

Money and success become a focus, and perhaps that is why they are there. We all exist for a different purpose, and we all fit together, in some way, shape, form, or fashion, in the gigantic puzzle of humanity. In the grand picture, when all the pieces fit together, the picture may appear differently for each of us.

Our minds will interpret things differently, and although our ears may hear the same sounds, and our eyes may see the same things, our minds will perceive those things differently based on our influences.

We are all quite unique, even while being the same.

"I want to be the next Stephen King," I said, as a young, aspiring author, years before writing a word in this book.

I was sitting in my mother and stepfather's kitchen, on a trip back north to visit them. My stepfather took a seat at the table opposite me, as I sat with my laptop, working on what would become my first novel.

"Hold on a second, Andy," he said. "You want to be the next Stephen King?"

I cleared my throat, sat back in the high back chair, and crossed my arms. "Yes," I said. "Do you remember the years when I worked at the campground? As the toll collector?"

He nodded. "Sure. Sure, I do."

"Well, you remember that I only had like two cars a day in that toll booth, right?"

He nodded.

388

"Well," I said. "I read some of his biggest works at that job. I think he is one of the authors who inspired me to become an author."

"I see."

I fidgeted in my chair. "Anne Rice too. I read *Interview with the Vampire* in popular reading in high school. I love her storytelling style and description. With my writing, I think, I could be the next Anne Rice."

He leaned forward and placed his arms on the table. He looked at me until I stared at him directly. "Can I give you some advice?"

I uncrossed my arms and sat back, nodding.

"I think it's great that you read their work. They're both amazing authors. Phenomenal storytellers. But why do you want to be the next version of them?"

I took a breath, raised my eyes and stared up towards the ceiling, and sighed.

After a few minutes, I lowered my head and looked across at him, staring at him directly. He was sitting there, waiting patiently, his eyebrows arched.

"They're both successful, as storytellers, and commercially," I said. "I have read both of their works.

They've inspired my writing, and my characters, and the worlds I write about."

"Andy, I need to tell you something important. And I hope you will listen to me. Because I know how much you love those authors. And if I cannot tell you anything else, I hope you will listen to this."

I nodded. "Of course, I will listen."

"Good," he said, as my mother brought a few cups of hot tea to the table. We each took a cup as he continued.

"Don't worry about being the next Stephen King," he said. "The world has that already. We all love his stories, and his movies, but we all have that. Your grandmother loved them, as you know."

"I do," I said.

"And don't be the next Anne Rice, either."

My mother settled into a chair next to her husband. "I know you really like Anne Rice," she said.

I nodded. "Sure. I love her description. And how she has carried her characters across novels and throughout the worlds she has created."

My stepfather leaned forward. "Look at me, Andy. You're a talented writer. You have a mind which many of us have not seen before. But why would you want to emulate other authors?"

I shifted in my chair, biting my lower lip.

I shrugged my shoulders. "They're successful. This is a hard business to break into."

He nodded and smiled. "Sure, they are! But you can be successful too. Not by emulating other authors, but by being *you* and who you are not only as a storyteller, but as a person. *Be the first A.L Mengel.* That is what the world needs, and that is what people want. They don't want another copycat author emulating their favorite authors. They want a new voice, someone different. Something they haven't seen or read before. Be the first A.L. Mengel, Andy!"

And those words resonated with me in the years to come.

I refused to let PKU hold me back from finding my journey in life. And I became increasingly thankful to my family, my mother, my father, my brother, and sisters, and all my siblings, and all of the others in my life who have helped guide me. They have helped shape my mind, not only into what it was destined to become, but also to what it may be.

Much credit goes to all the angels who were placed in my life to protect me from what could have been a disastrous effect on my mind and well-being. The diet is for life, and the three letters which follow me around will always be waiting for me in the shadows. Even without the watchful eyes of my family, who have all become experts themselves on the condition, I still, to this day, have days when things don't always go so well.

It was never an intentional rebellion against the restrictions, or a desire to cheat and explore new foods, like it was in high school. Days which come, as an adult, when I would exceed my allowable allotment of protein, would come as unintentional.

I now am very aware of the effects of increased levels of blood phenylalanine; skin conditions, irritability, and the difficulty I would have with concentration and focus. I may be chronologically well beyond the years and fears of mental hindrance, but I have learned to listen to my body, as many of us do.

I can tell when things have gotten away from me for a bit. For the effects of PKU do, as always, come like a thief in the night.

Despite those challenges, I have consciously worked to overcome the obstacles that have remained with me throughout my adult life and worked to scale the hurdles which have presented themselves to me. Possibly due to a result of increased scrutiny while young. I must consciously be aware of my addictive personality, as well as my blood and test phobias.

$$\mathcal{LL}$$

In 2017, when I was writing *The Europa Effect,* I was writing it with a tissue hanging out of my mouth.

I had it wedged between the sides of my teeth, chewing on it slightly. Because it would ease the pain. One of my back molars was probably abscessed. Gums started swelling up on me the other day.

And so, I was there, typing on the manuscript, telling my outer space story, chewing on a sloppy, wet, white tissue, wishing I hadn't ignored my oral health for so many years.

But it's not like I didn't brush my teeth. I was taught well. I have a beautiful smile, perfectly straight teeth thanks to my time with braces, yet, as a adult, I developed a fear, perhaps brought on by some mild hypochondria, and it took writing my novel *The Quest for Immortality* to help channel those fears onto the page, and carry me past the demons which cast my thoughts into dark places, piercing my mind with negative energy, making me believe that every little problem was more than it was.

I did take care of my teeth. And do, of course. But for some time, I feared going to the dentist. I didn't have any sort of specific reason, except that my anxiety would gnaw at my insides, developing a belief that I stayed away for too long, and the results of the x-ray would be grim, of course.

I knew I had a cavity.

My tooth was bothering me, and the tissue helped ease the pain. As I typed furiously, as the story for *The Europa Effect* poured out of me, I was able to put reality aside for a while.

The following morning, I was sitting in the dentist's chair, and the x-rays were not as devastating as I dreaded. Yes, I needed some dental work. But putting it off was not something I should have done, but it was what it was.

But that is what happens when one doesn't pay close enough attention to health concerns. And there are so many different health questions that all of us must address every day.

I'm also on blood pressure medication, thanks to genetics. That's another one that I've shied away from over the years.

"I have white coat hypertension," my younger self would tell a nodding doctor as my blood pressure reading would be indicative of a prescription. But I would randomly float from doctor to doctor, in-between internet searches for anything I was experiencing that might be considered a symptom.

I didn't know it then.

But I know it now.

I was, it seemed, a full-fledged badge wearing hypochondriac.

It's not that I would manifest symptoms that weren't there. They were *real.* The tissue that was hanging out of my mouth was *real.* I could taste its dry and papery perfume in my mouth. And when I reposition it when the twisted end gets soaked with my saliva, I could feel it with my fingers.

Completely real.

It existed.

So, I wasn't a complete hypochondriac, was I?

When I went to the doctor with a random questionable stomach rash when I was in my twenties, it was real. I remember it. And I recall the panic when I woke up with it one morning, lifting my t-shirt, as a young twenty-something, and gasping. "Oh my god! I have some horrible infection!" I exclaimed to my friend on the phone.

"Just see the doctor," he said. "Get some cream."

Talking to others would provide some temporary respite from my panicked outbursts, as my mind shifted, automatically, to the worst-case scenario: "Well then. *Clearly,* I have contracted some devastating disease! It could be a fungal infection!" My friend scoffed. The conversation quickly turned to other topics, but I still had the topic of my stomach rash on my mind.

I mustered up courage.

I knew I had a doctor.

I didn't know him very well, but I'd seen him once for a physical, months previously. And that was the relationship I'd had at that stage in my life, in my twenties.

I saw the doctor religiously, and regularly, until I reached my mid-twenties, and then, I stopped wanting to go.

I found the glory of the internet and made a feeble attempt to manage my own health and self-diagnose my symptoms. My PKU was still in the background, and aside from my anxieties, I seemed to be doing well. I was living my life over a thousand miles from my home and the protection of my family. I was renting an apartment, leasing a car. I had jobs and friends, overall felt like I was a happy person in those years.

Yet I remember avoiding mirrors.

Perhaps I was at a stage of my life when I was experiencing myself getting older.

And my body was changing.

My face started looking different to me. New lines were developing that I couldn't remember being there before, no matter how hard I tried. I kept asking myself – was I getting sick? Was there something going on that I wasn't aware of?

I had thoughts in my mind that I was losing weight, unintentionally, yet when I look back on that period of my life, when I was losing my baby face, and making the transition to a more adult bone structure, I was not losing weight at all.

If anything, I was gaining weight.

I was not used to seeing myself looking older. Perhaps I was being vain, or possibly I was clinging to my youth as it slipped through my fingers, but now, looking back at that period of my life, I realize that I was experiencing exactly what I needed to for the plot of *The Quest for Immortality* to develop. The book follows an immortal who drinks a potion which robs him of his gift, and he becomes mortal once again. In the story, he is searching for an elixir to grant him the gift once again, as he is rapidly aging, his body catching up to his soul.

I was so concerned about wasting away, that I would shovel food down my throat when I wasn't even hungry. They were all allowable foods for PKU, but I gave no regard for measuring. For I was concerned about getting smaller.

I had seen some friends become sick and lose weight at that point, and I was starting to understand my mortality. PKU was there, I was drinking my formula regularly and was grateful for its nourishment.

But I felt I could not measure my food or restrict myself. For I would look in the mirror, and see every small line that developed, thinking it was the start of some devastating disease.

My lower back broke out in a horrendous yet painless red rash.

It did not bother me, because I knew exactly what it was.

During those days, I knew that my blood phenylalanine level was high. For it was the same eczema I experienced when I was younger. I was overeating, every day, day in and day out. But I had to keep my weight up. I had not seen a doctor at that point for quite some time, and now, I had really done it.

Doctor's visits were rushed and incomplete, and I focused on whatever symptom I was experiencing at the time, and I did not let the doctor review anything else or perform any other tests. I could not be chastised for what I was doing.

"But I'm not cheating!"

I reached up and wiped the condensation from the mirror. I was still wearing the towel from my shower. "You have to stop this. Overeating can raise your blood levels. And you know it. You are destroying your body. See a doctor! Get your shit together!"

I rested my palms on the counter and hung my head down. "If you want to be an author," I said, looking back into the mirror, staring at myself directly. "You have to *stop destroying your fucking mind!*"

CHAPTER NINETEEN

So why, then, am I here? Why are any of us here?

Simply to live, get sick, and die?

When one has a condition that requires significant medical intervention, whether it be something like PKU, or another incurable condition that has to be managed on a lifelong basis without any help for relief, one can ask that question. Why was I placed here? Simply to endure these hardships?

People have looked up towards the cosmos, wondering about the existence beyond, for millennia. Perhaps it could be for a search for purpose or asking benevolent beings why so much suffering is endured on the surface below.

I am swiftly approaching fifty as I now write in this book.

What is my purpose?

As I have been attempting to take all that I have written over the years, and make some sense out of it, and organize it, and form my thoughts and memories into a story that will flow and provide some much needed clarification on what Phenylketonuria is, and why it can be important, not only to manage it effectively so as not to have emotional, relationship, financial, and legal problems, but also why it is important for others to understand the disorder and recognize the need for support to those who have PKU.

For most of my life, I have been early to bed and early to rise, and as I move through middle age, I have become quite deeply connected with the mornings, the sunrise, and nature. It seems to be an hour of the day that I am most spiritually connected with, but I do not mean that in a religious sense.

It is a sense of connectedness, those early mornings with the wildlife and the sky gazing. Casting thoughts outwards, beyond our physical limitations. An expansion of the mind towards distant realms, to where any sense of exactness simply fades away.

My mind is also very scientific, and I have much respect for others who do not share the same values as I do. As well as those who do. I think we were all placed on this earth, not to be homogenous in the very least. We were meant to be diverse; we were meant to have different belief systems, or to not believe in anything at all.

Yet I continue my journey towards the mountaintop, to view the clouds, to be bathed in light, to attain a closeness with something greater than myself.

When I think about why I am here, I think back to the stepping stones.

And the ocean waves; the sea spray crashing against them, and the feeling of trepidation when I attempt to muster the effort to make it to the next stone.

PKU can be an easy scapegoat.

I used to complain to my family that sometimes the irritability, and the symptoms of elevated blood phenylalanine, can also mimic basic human emotion. I explained to them that sometimes I was just upset about something, and that I was experiencing that emotion from something else, rather than cheating on my diet.

403

But they knew.

Sometimes, I was telling the truth. In my teenage years, it was a lie. As an adult, I have moved beyond actively cheating. But I still have bad days.

When I did something wrong, somehow.

And many other times, my discouragement, my irritability, my argumentativeness, were very much a result of not eating correctly.

While I have not actively cheated on the diet in my adult years, I have a tendency to sometimes overeat, and even when I cook, which I have become quite proficient at, I do like to sample to learn the balance of flavors, spices, and sauces.

It's not the sampling that can throw my blood levels off balance.

When I pay less attention to what I am eating throughout the course of the day, or when I eat too much of the foods I am able to have, my blood phenylalanine can build up.

And although now, as a middle-aged man, the effects on my mind will not be the same as it would have been when I was a child, I can still experience irritability, struggles with concentration and focus, as well as judgement impairment and skin issues.

When I was a child, my mother used to scour the supermarket to find foods that could be considered "free" (which is what she called them) so I could eat, and eat, and eat, and not have to pay so close attention to what I was eating. But in my experience, I have learned that nothing is really "free".

My father also did quite a bit, especially in the days when I was living with my stepfamily in the summertime. I remember dinners which were planned around my dietary restrictions; everyone ate more vegetables and salads as a result, regardless of whether we dined at home or in restaurants. But like my mother's quest to find "free" foods, everything, really, has a degree of protein in it, and therefore has phenylalanine as well.

Everything must be counted, and it doesn't matter what it is.

That will be the cross I continue to bear, until the day I die, unless a cure for PKU is found.

While my childhood now seems to be in the distant past, I have learned much from it, particularly with the writing of this book. If one were to divide my life into stages, the first decade would be the years when I was told what to do and what to eat, and I followed everything I was told to do.

When I was trying to establish my medical care in a different city, I touched my mom's name on the phone screen and brought it up to my ear. With each ring, my anxiety increased. I loved chatting with her, and I felt compelled to remain in touch.

But I knew, as I called her in desperation for a resource for additional PKU formula to get my protein, that I was making this her problem far after it should have been.

In those days, with each time I called came an increasing level of apprehension, which would crescendo with each ring.

But this was my mother.

She was the furthest from being judgmental. She would never do that. The only goal was to make sure that I was okay and had everything that I needed. And I knew that the formula was running low.

I turned and looked at the small carboard boxes in the pantry. Down to one. She picked up the phone and I heard a familiar, warm voice.

"You are low on formula again?" she asked after a few minutes of conversation. "How has it been going with finding a PKU clinic down there?"

I paused.

She knew.

There hadn't been much of a cause to my destiny, at least that's what I had thought. I had left my childhood home, all of the friends I had made up to that point in my life and took the next step on my journey.

Those first stepping-stones were hard; they were slippery.

And I would frequently fall off, and downwards, seemingly through the clouds through an endless dark sky, as the thoughts pierced my mind, wondering when I would hit the ground.

But the ground never came.

There was always someone there. The hand that reached from the sky, downwards, to rescue me. I caught my breath and felt the strength pull me up. I could feel the tenseness in my muscles lessen as I flung myself back on the stone.

I was rescued.

"I have some cases of your formula at the house," mom said. "I can send a few cases down to you."

Hastily, I agreed.

"But you have to go back to the clinic, Andrew. You have to get your blood tested. When was the last time you went to the doctor?"

I let out an exasperated sigh. "I have *told* you, mom. *No clinic will take me.* Not down here. I have called so many times. They always ask me, 'have you been in a pediatric PKU program here?' And then of course, I say no. And then they say they can only see me if I have been in a pediatric program *with them*."

"That doesn't make any sense, Andrew."

"But that is what they are telling me! And, yes, I do go to the doctor, mom. I told my doctor that I had PKU on my last visit, and he stared at me like I had three heads."

"It's the clinic, Andrew. You have to see the specialist. The general practitioner isn't going to be that well versed in PKU. That's what the clinic and the dieticians are for. And the blood tests."

I scoffed.

"I know my body. I know when my level is up."

I held the phone closer to my ear as mom continued. "You can't always know, Andrew. You need the blood tests to see where you're at."

I shivered and closed my eyes.

In my mind I saw the bathroom in the house when I was growing up, and I walked slowly through the door as if I was an unseen spirit, walking along the white tiles, unobserved.

There was mom. So much younger in those days.

I was sitting on her lap, still a young boy. I watched my younger self as I stood in the center of the bathroom as my mom cradled me next to the toilet. I watched as she put her arms around me, and saw tears stream down my little cheeks.

As I stood in the center of the bathroom floor, watching myself and watching my mother, I knew why I felt that I knew my body so well.

I looked at the scene. I was so brave as a child, even as I remembered my heart beating fast when I saw the reflection of the sharp lancet catching the light.

I saw the boy's eyes widen and the pained look on her face. My mother had no choice but to stab my finger with it. I'm certain that she hated hurting her little boy, but there was no choice in the matter.

The level had to be checked.

"No, no *no!*"

I watched as I squealed and squirmed in her arms and looked at the wide eyes and terror on my face as a boy.

I could no longer endure it.

The blood.

There was too much of it, throughout my life.

From the finger stabs to the vein punctures in my arm there was always blood. And so many tests. The bright crimson liquid which flowed from my veins, and my fingers, and became the fluid I feared. I would stare at red, viscous liquid, and question if the test results would come back as they should.

Or what others expected them to be.

Ironically, *The Blood Decanter* helped me move past that blood phobia I once had, as I rained that crimson fear onto the pages of an epic supernatural thriller, allowing me to move forward, and grant myself medical help once again.

CHAPTER TWENTY

Expectations are something that can motivate us to improve ourselves, yet, at the same time, they can also hold us back, cause us to retreat to our comfort zones, and to question our ability to make it to that next stone on our journeys.

Many of us focus on the expectations others place on us.

I am guilty of that.

I walked through my life, worried about what others would think of me. I would blame PKU – my condition – on any shortcomings I would experience. But those types of pitfalls, I have found, are simply the tiny holes in the stones on our path, which remain part of our journey regardless of what we may do to prevent them.

"I am not going to Hell," I said to a friend. "I didn't choose a life of sin. This life chose *me*. I can't help but think, sometimes, that I serve as a catalyst for others to better understand the things which cannot be so easily interpreted."

"What do you mean? Can you clarify?"

I nodded and took a sip from my mug.

"It's all about the physical world versus what we cannot see," I said, placing my cup back down and straightening myself in my chair. "As an author, I have been the subject of ridicule and misunderstanding. Not everyone understands my work or even wants to."

I watched him as his eyebrows raised.

"Really?"

I nodded. "Comments came to my social media channels, and it's quite interesting how people who are in your life can so easily turn their backs on you. At that point in my life, I was a new author. This was my third book. *The Blood Decanter.* The most A.L. Mengely title I had written at that point. I remember a conversation I had during that time period, about being my own unique self. Even in my writing. And I've stuck with that. Do they like me?"

"Who?" my friend asked.

I shrugged my shoulders.

"The people who follow me," I said. "And who read my books. Some of them have been commenting on my page like they didn't like my book."

He took a quick sip of his beer, set the glass down, and looked at me, making direct eye contact. "You are A.L. Mengel," he said. "Just because some people don't like your work, doesn't mean you should change it."

There is something liberating, yet terrifying, about sharing oneself with the world.

I make sure to project an image of confidence when I engage with my readers, or YouTube viewers, as I learned that image is meaningful. Yet still, underneath, I have the same vulnerabilities as many do. I still catch myself, sometimes, hiding my PKU from the world. But it truly is a journey. One that will always be in the back of my mind.

Would someone, in the twenty-first century, truly care about what I could or could not eat?

Have you ever sat and had a conversation with a complete stranger? Maybe it was by chance, or perhaps it was meant to be carved into the destiny of your own journey, but do you remember a conversation that you had with someone you didn't know which transformed you in some way? Or motivate you in some way?

I have had many of those conversations.

Safe from harm.

That was the song I most remembered from Miami.

When I was in my apartment in the downtown high-rise in Miami, I remember hearing the beat and melody from a club anthem from the nightclub district which was a mere few blocks away. I learned later that it was the song "Safe from Harm" by a musical group called Narcotic Thrust. And years later, I remembered my journey, through the darkness, experiencing a respite.

Angels have always been placed in my life, in one form, or another.

Andrew's mind must be protected. There is never an option to fail.

Years after I lived in Miami, after meeting my best and closest friend, while living in our small, rented apartment, I finally was able to focus, with his encouragement, and finish my first novel. My first Beta reader.

"Hey!" I said. "Hey, come here. You have to see this."

My best friend emerged from the adjoining room of our shared apartment. "What is it, Andy?"

I shifted my body in the chair and pointed at the small computer monitor.

His mouth dropped open and his eyes widened. "You're finished?!"

I smiled and nodded.

I could feel tears well up within my eyes as I felt a tickle in my throat. This was it. A break in the journey. I didn't know what would come next, but I know that I had finally accomplished something that many could not.

I completed my first novel.

"You kept the title?"

I shook my head. "You mean *The Last Nail in the Coffin*? No. It's *Ashes*. Like we talked about, and you suggested. I think that is the best title."

"Yes, it is," he said. "Just that one word. *Ashes*. It can have so many different meanings. And it really grabs you."

I turned my head and looked at the monitor, staring at the two words I had been wanting to write for many years. *The End*.

It was a reason to celebrate, indeed.

PART SIX

WHERE AM I GOING?

CHAPTER TWENTY-ONE

There they were.

The planets, perfectly aligned, in plain view, without a telescope. I looked down at my dog, as she raised her head towards me, her eyes wide, large brown circles. *I am here to protect you now.*

Mercury, Venus, Mars, Jupiter, and Saturn.

It was like nothing I had ever seen before.

I had taken the dog out for her early morning walk earlier than I ever had, but she always enjoyed it, even if the sky was still dark, and the stars were still guarding us like sentinels, and if the ducks were not yet out waddling around the lake.

We walked under the early morning sky, as the cosmos bathed us in their beauty.

I remembered the letters.

When I would skip out to the mailbox as a little boy, eager to receive that next letter from my pen pal, my aunt. I looked up at the plants, the small spheres which stretched across the sky.

I know you are still out there. I know you are still with us.

They all are.

Yet I have found, as I would look up towards the sky, especially thoughtful while gazing towards a masterful and cosmic painting, whether it be then or at the sunrise, or a sunset, we can find those who we've lost. For that is where they reside. And we also can guide ourselves, throughout our lives, to respect what we have been taught to allow us more time to exist in this world.

We are all on the same journey.

I would always think that.

No one knew, especially myself, that I would have a talent for writing. And even along the way, after *Ashes* was published, there were days when I would become discouraged. And also, when my thoughts would cast themselves off the page and into my daily life.

While in my thirties, after my house was robbed, I became obsessed with home security. While the break in was real, I remember hammering two by fours into the sides of the window frames to deter potential criminals from jacking a window open (our window was broken as a way to enter the house).

That also was a time before we had a home security system, and cameras, and various means of protection. *Ashes* was finished but not yet published, and after my first novel went into publication, I noticed periods when thoughts of despair would cast themselves into my mind.

It's okay, Andrew. You're allowed to have a bad day.

And it is during these times that sometimes, when I have feelings of paranoia, or irritability, or discouragement, that it really is just basic human emotion, and maybe even more so because I have the mind of an author.

It isn't to say that my mind is trained to imagine the worst (because it is, at least for my fiction) and I have had numerous conversations with my mother, particularly on days when I am frustrated, or mad at the world.

"Andrew, you really need to read the book *The Power of Positive Thinking*."

I shook my head, even though we were on the phone, over a thousand miles between us, and there was no way she could see it. "No, no. It doesn't work."

Maybe she could picture me sitting in the rocking chair on the lanai, my dogs at my feet, as I cradled the phone between my ear and shoulder, allowing me to fold my arms in protest.

"It *does* work, Andrew. Just think positively! Look at that amazing award you won. Your author career has expanded well beyond what I imagined. Your mind is such an amazing thing. Few people write books, especially the way that you do."

I sat and held the phone and knew she was right. "Maybe it's true," I said.

"Yes, it is," she said. "Think positively. And good things will happen."

And it really is okay.

I am allowed to have a bad day, just as we all are. It does happen from time to time, and PKU doesn't always need to be the scapegoat. Still, I sometimes wish I had the courage to agree with my mother verbally as often as the encouragement is given. Perhaps, one day, I will. I do sometimes, but there are those days that I know I need to hear it said to me, even if I am not agreeing verbally in that moment.

Because she is right.

She always has been.

When I was growing up, she knew. Everyone knew when I was out of sorts. When I was a teenager, everyone knew I was cheating on the diet.

And even now, as an adult, she still knows when things are off.

I imagine she could tell, even though we were speaking on the phone, if my bloodwork numbers were elevated. Because discouragement would seem to take over.

It wasn't really me.

And the angels in my life, and time, can carry me back to positiveness.

I would sit there talking with her, knowing it in my head, yet I would still hear myself speaking differently, drowning in a pool of despair. She would always toss me the life preserver, the hand would appear to straighten me on the stone, to help me up the steep mountain.

The help was there.

She and the other angels have had power to force me to reach out for that helping hand.

The PKU diet is meticulous, particularly during current times, now that we know it works.

When I am managing it as an adult, the challenges no longer come from having a foul-tasting formula to drink for nutrition – the formulas now cater to the working adult. In many cases, they come pre-made and pre-measured, for a busy, on-the-go lifestyle.

And the formulas now actually taste *good*.

I look forward to sipping on them, as they are now more like smoothies. They bring me sustenance, and I always feel better when drinking them properly.

As a more seasoned author, I venture out into the world with my laptop in tow and write outside the house so I can observe and experience the world. But most importantly, with people.

With a period of easier ordering at restaurants, not only for PKU, but many other conditions which warrant a restricted diet, restaurants that are more cognitive of special dietary restrictions have been capturing an increased level of business.

I enjoyed writing and eating out and about. And, as I would write, and examine, and explore the questions that we all have, I would observe.

People.

And what we all do. And how we are. And how we feel.

As I would look around the room, I would watch all the people around me. The older, overweight man shoving fried food into his mouth. The middle-aged man nursing a drink and looking downwards, studying his phone. The young couple sitting close by, seemingly with years ahead of them; her hair dyed pink, a look of inexperience on his face.

It's uncanny how things can be unpredictable, uncertain, all the time.

Any one of us could be lying in a casket by next week. And it may not be the older man gorging on fried food. It could be one of the members of the young couple, or anyone. The bartender. Someone in the parking lot.

Or me.

None of us know. Nor should we want to, as our steppingstones continue their reach outwards, towards the horizon, until we can no longer see their destination.

Life is precious.

I've thought a lot about this book, and who it is about.

Who it really is about. And I could always say myself, but that would be selfish and self-serving. There is no way that I would be able to exist the way that I am existing today without the others in my life who have helped me on this journey, and the daily uncertainties which I continue to face.

Is PKU really all that bad of a condition?

I don't think so, to be honest.

Those three letters have always been a part of me. When I tell people about PKU, sometimes they look at the parameters, and gasp. And maybe for others who don't have those types of restrictions can't imagine life with those types of limitations, and they say that to me. "I don't know how you live with that," they say. "I couldn't live like that."

I would always shrug my shoulders. "It's just the way it's always been."

They tend to nod. "A lot of respect for that," they say. "I don't know how you do it."

But to me, all of the things that I have had to deal with concerning PKU are simply part of my day. Do I dream of a time when there is a cure?

Sure, I do.

But that cross sure has lost some weight.

LL

I think, frequently, of the mountain top.

How challenging it can be to scale, reaching hands out to grab at steep rock, as the terrain below becomes increasingly threatening.

What if I were to fall?

I grab the stone in front of me, feeling its rough surface. The light would shine, nearly blinding me. But I knew it was friendly, and wanted me to succeed, to find my purpose, to discover my destiny.

When I lifted my arm up, I grabbed the pointed stone. It was cool and ridged. I had to muster that last bit of strength to get there. I'd carried the cross for so long, on such a lengthy journey. It felt so heavy; sometimes I would place it on my shoulder. My face grimaced. It couldn't be that heavy. But maybe it was.

I raised my head, looking up towards the top of the mountain, concealed in a puffy white blanket of

427

clouds. Can I get up there? Up above the clouds, and the darkness, and experience the warmth and light?

The voices rang through my head.

Why are you so different?

You eat weird!

Your house is so hot. I only stayed there because my mom made me.

Come on. Let's get you to the hospital. No one should have vision like that.

We were all just figuring it out, Andrew. No one knew if this would work.

I had to breast feed you, so your mind would develop normally. It was not an option to fail…

I closed my eyes, drawing my lower lip inwards under my teeth, holding on the pointed stone with all of my might. My heart pounded in my chest, and I knew, deep within myself, that this was the precise moment to overcome these fears.

I raised my head, opened my eyes and looked upwards at the swirling, white clouds.

I took a deep breath, and reached upwards, my hand disappearing into the cloud cover. I reached around, desperately in search of the next rock I could grab onto.

And then I felt the warmth of a hand.

It took my hand, wrapping its strength around mine, and it lifted me upwards to the top of the mountain, through the clouds, into the sky, in view of the bright and brilliant warmth of the sun.

When I was child, I had a dream that when I died, I would arrive in Heaven, and there would be a long table, reaching so far into the billowing, white, pillowy clouds that I could not see the end of the table. There would be large, elegant chairs lining the sides, with high backs, as if fit for royalty. There would be a massive banquet, filled with many different foods.

The table was set with the most glorious and delicious looking foods; all the types of foods that I was never permitted to eat. There would be large racks of lamb, ham and turkey, gigantic bowls of stuffing, and hot dogs, sausages and cheese filled pierogies and pizza. Steaming bowls of macaroni and cheese and cakes and pies and custard.

My family would appear, pulling out the chairs, sitting down, and welcoming me to the table. I would recognize my mother; she would smile, beaming in front of me, elated to see her beloved son once again. "We have been waiting for you, Andrew," she would say. My father would stand next to us, and we would all be together as a family once again, and the extended family, and the spouses and step brothers and sisters would be there as well, all pulling out chairs, and preparing for the very special meal.

I would raise my head, looking up, seeing the smiling faces looking down at me, so very familiar. I knew that my entire life had prepared me for this moment. I had been destined for the journey which was chosen specifically for me. The cross I was given was not a mistake. It was an intention that must be carried through to the end.

I would look at the table, and watch my family, patiently waiting for me to take my place at the head of the table. The presences which surrounded me guided the largest chair outwards from the table, as they ushered me to sit in front of so many glorious and delicious foods which I had been so long denied.

I looked over at my mother, who nodded, and smiled, and my father, who was on the opposite side of the table. And next to them was my brother, and sisters, and their children and spouses, and my step parents and their children, and their cousins, and aunts, and uncles, and their spouses and their children and grandparents, and their parents and their grandparents and more cousins and aunts and uncles…reaching outwards into the pillowy white.

"Welcome Andrew," they said. "This is all for you. All prepared in celebration of your arrival. Now sit with us, and eat, as much as you want. Eat whatever you want."

THE END

Three Letters is a true story in production from 2007 to 2025. I invite you to continue reading the letters and resources in the following sections of the book.

2007 - June 6, 2023, A.L. Mengel (first run)

September 2, 2023, A.L. Mengel (second run)

September 14, 2025 (final run)

PART SEVEN

THE THREE LETTERS

CHAPTER TWENTY-TWO

The *Three Letters* story, as you read it, encompasses the timeline of my life from birth until the publication of my first novel, *Ashes*, with a focus on PKU, the development of my mind, and some of the other conditions that I have dealt with – whether it be anxiety or phobias or other – as a possible result of my PKU. This story was far from an autobiography, as there are far more aspects of my life that would have to be covered in that type of written work.

Still, I do not yet believe that I have accomplished enough yet, in my life, to warrant an autobiography, despite the development thus far of my author career.

It would have been impossible, without the intervention of my parents, family, closest friends, and medical team, for me to have achieved the level of success as an author that I have. While no one knew what the end result would be, the result was extraordinary. I genuinely attribute it to my parents, and particularly my mother, and their insistence that I be breast fed. That allowed my brain, and my mind, to not only develop normally, but also in a rather unique and extraordinary way.

I am currently drinking three different PKU formulas, which are manufactured by Cambrooke Foods out of Massachusetts, USA. I have two Ready to Drink formulas (15 grams of protein each) that are in small boxes and can be consumed at room temperature (but taste best when refrigerated). I chose the flavors – Café Mocha and Vanilla – and I can sip of them throughout the day, with or without meals, and have up to three daily which gives my body up to 45 grams of protein.

Due to my challenges in finding a PKU specific program, which was touched on in the story you just read, I have been treating my PKU in an unorthodox way – via my General Practitioner. "We are going to help you manage your PKU," she told me, as I was sitting in the exam room with her. "I don't understand why you have had such a hard time getting into a PKU program, but I am a doctor. And I understand nutrition."

And just like that, I was back in the system.

That is how the stepping stones in my journey took a direction that I never thought they would take. For the longest time, I thought I was lost in the system, and I didn't know if – or how – I would be able to start my PKU treatment again as it was meant to be. Before I left for Florida, when I left home for the first time, was the last time I was seen by a PKU specialist. Despite continuing to follow the diet, and drink the medically prescribed formulas, many years passed as an adult from when I was seen by a specialist, and a nutritionist, and had my blood tested.

I think I had reached a point when I wasn't quite so lost.

I just got off a phone call with my mother, and we were discussing some of the things that appeared in the story you just read. I made a comment and surprised myself. "Mom, you know. There are four PKU clinics within three hours of my house. There is one in Orlando, another in Tampa, one in Jacksonville, and another in Miami."

Yet she knows the brick walls I have been hitting.

"We are a pediatric program," they would all say. "You would have to have been our patient since you were a child."

And the journey continued, yet for years, without visiting an actual clinic.

As a young adult, I had started to avoid going to the doctor, as often as possible, because often, when I went to the doctor, it would trigger intense anxiety, particularly for fear of being bad. Was I doing the things I wasn't supposed to? Was I eating the things that I wasn't supposed to eat?

I didn't think so.

Throughout my adult life, I have actively worked to eat the foods that I am able to eat, and have experienced better health, I would imagine, as a result. Still, the PKU diet can also be disrupted by amounts. I remember explaining to others, when they would ask why I could have sour cream or gravy. "It's about amounts and protein density," I would say. "I can't sit down and eat an entire piece of chicken. My blood levels would be completely screwed up. But I can drizzle the drippings on my potatoes like everyone else."

"I don't understand that. Aren't you allergic to all that?"

I would nod. "Of course, yes. But my body can tolerate a certain amount. I can try pretty much anything. But I can't have an entire meal of it. I pretty much have to stick to fruits and vegetables, my special low protein breads and pastas, and I drink a doctor prescribed formula to get the protein my body needs without the things my body cannot process."

"It sounds like a lot to manage."

I would always shrug my shoulders. "At one point, it sure was. Mainly talking to my parents. I was just a baby. A little kid. I didn't know about all of the anxiety they had. I was just a kid, and things were how they were."

"Wow…so you have to deal with a bunch of anxiety now?"

"I still have anxiety, but I am much better able to manage it," I would reply. "The diet itself has gotten much easier over the years. It's been proven that it works. And that people have to be on it for life, unless there is some miraculous cure. The PKU babies that are born these days have many more options. They have PKU hot dogs, and chicken tenders, and cheese."

They would nod.

"Sure, kids need to fit in, don't they?"

439

And then I would pause in the new conversation that would always take place.

As a middle-aged man, I would always think about my being different, and my quest to do so. But I would think back to the little boy, who was always eating fruits and salads, and cheering for juice that the other kids ignored. And I knew the reason why the PKU foods were made to resemble the forbidden foods.

I would raise my eyes to them, looking at them directly. "They sure do."

To my siblings,

There were so many things that I remember from when we were growing up.

I imagine that your minds were just as wondering as mine as to why Andrew needed the special diet and foods, but we all needed to manage. And with all of you, it seemed like the PKU didn't matter, but sometimes it did. I remember my little sister eating my powdered formula from the cannister with a spoon because it was sweet and she loved it, and she had a sweet tooth.

I watched her in horror as I thought the formula was disgusting, but I had it after it was mixed with water, and as a replacement for the other foods which I always wanted to have. Regardless, she always loved it. I am uncertain if she still likes is now, that we are all middle-aged, but images of her eating it with a spoon out of the can are cemented in my mind.

I also remember summers at the lake, and whenever I smell a charcoal grill, it reminds me of our outdoor cookouts, and those were always fun to have, sitting and swinging our legs at the old, rickety wooden picnic tables, with our towels wrapped around our waists, and our hair still mussed and wet from the lake. We used to eat as fast as we could because the old navy blue and red "leemoraft" was waiting for us on the beach. And Pierre Bonnee would have to be leemoed around by his siblings.

I remember my other siblings, when our parents remarried, who also were their own part of the journey. I remember playing barbies, as a young boy, with one of the stepsisters with whom I was quite close in age.

Do any of you remember when we got those corsage and boutonniere containers (the small clear ones) and when I saw a long, rectangular one, I held it up to dad. "Hey Dad, look! It's a Barbie coffin!"

Everyone rolled their eyes at me, of course. But no one more than dad. He rolled his eyes and shook his head. "I'm gonna Barbie coffin you."

When I look back, I am now older than he was when he made that joke.

We dashed around and had fun hanging in the Gravatron at the Festival when we were in high school with our stepdad's daughter, who was also close in age to me as well. And who doesn't remember Mom rolling around on the floor when we played Charades and she was trying to get us to guess *The Poseidon Adventure*?

Memories like these, which we often tend to forget with the passage of time, remind us of why we want to catch time somehow, in some way. We've all tried to capture time. But when I stare at the darkened skies at night, I think about all of you, living in distant locations, and separate lives. I know that something in our destinies drew us each to separate journeys in different, faraway places, but my mind preserves our connections.

I remain close to you in thought, and, I know, when we meet up and see each other in person, however sporadic it may be, that those days, the long-ago times when we were laughing and playing together, when we played fort and army in the woods behind the house. When we walked together to the penny candy store after school, when we went out to the Chinese restaurant together as a family and we would order vegetable delight, hot and spicy, like Dad always did.

When we went to the festival and sat on the Ferris Wheel together, swinging the car; when we mowed and wrestled in the lawn at the place we jokingly called "Fart ' n' run"; when we roller skated in the basement blasting music, when we slid down the stairs in laundry baskets, when we drove to Cape May in my first car that kept stalling, when I fell into the cactus in Tucson, when I gave a drunken yet fun toast in New Orleans, when we got together to say goodbye to our grandparents.

Considered it all captured.

With Love,

Andrew

To my Father,

One of the things I most remember was that over the decades, we always have remained close.

I think a lot of it comes from your being my father, and you, along with my mother, were the primary catalysts for allowing me to live a normal life. I remember when you took us all the McDonald's, and we sat at a table in the corner.

I had an orange drink, because that is what I loved. You sat with the three of us and said that you had to move away. It was the only time in my life that I had seen you cry. When you said you had to leave, you started sobbing, and I understood why we were in a discreet location in the restaurant, back by the bathrooms.

You knew, and by your knowing, you shielded us from the public who may not understand why a man was crying in front of his children.

When I saw that, your vulnerability came through, and I knew the move was something you had worked hard not to do. But there was no choice in the matter.

You have always been one of the strongest figures in my life.

I remember when I spoke to my older stepsister, and she pulled me aside once, and told me how proud you were of me. Especially now as a published author, and I was elated to hear that. I know the direction I have taken in life may have been different than you may have thought, and I never really had the brilliant business mind that you and others in my life have, but I have harnessed my power with a creative mind.

Knowing that you were proud of me for it has been life changing.

And I thank you, Dad, for the role that you have played in my life.

I thank you for your role in my care, and the development of my mind, and for all of the times you took me to MCL for the vegetable plate, and all the times you ran to the store to get me a portobello mushroom to put on the grill. And all the times we shared a bourbon or a beer together.

I am forever indebted to you for allowing me to live this life.

Love,

Your son, Andrew

To My Mother,

Without your perseverance in the way you raised me, I would not have been able to live the life I am living today.

Pure and simple.

There really is no other way to slice it, you have become the hero of my story. After researching and writing this book, I firmly believe that it was the insistence of breast milk that has allowed my mind to develop into what it has become today.

I don't know how the others with PKU are doing, the children who were also placed on the experimental diet around the same time I was; how they turned out. I wonder sometimes, if they were taken off diet around the same time that the doctors approached you and said I could be taken off diet.

And I wonder if their parents had taken them off the diet.

Yet even so, even if their parents had kept them on the PKU diet just as diligently as you all did, I sometimes also wonder if those babies were breast fed. Or if they were simply bottle fed. I wonder how their minds have developed. And they may be doing just fine; they may be extraordinary.

One thing I know, however, is certain.

You kept me on the treatment.

And I was breast fed. And along with the rest of the family, you spearheaded the development of my mind, all the way to winning my Gold Medal award for Best Supernatural Fiction for my thirteenth book. And for that, I am eternally grateful.

If it wasn't for you holding me in the bathroom when I was terrified of the lancet; or when I was gasping for air in the middle of the night, I don't think I would have gotten to the point where I am today. If you hadn't made me cut the cigarettes in half, or if you hadn't spent your weekends creating recipes that not only could I eat, but the rest of the family could enjoy as well, then I don't believe my journey would have had the same result. You helped me get to the top of the mountain. And to my family as well, I thank you all for it.

This mind you all built is just as much yours as it is mine.

Love,

Andrew.

Three Letters.

THREE

LETTERS

Please leave a book review. Follow A.L. Mengel on social media and take a journey through his other books of award winning supernatural and science fiction.

www.ingramcontent.com/pod-product-compliance
Lightning Source LLC
Chambersburg PA
CBHW030714110426
42739CB00029B/60